Gui

SONATAS

Also by Melvin Berger

GUIDE TO CHAMBER MUSIC

Guide to
SONATAS

Music for One or Two Instruments

MELVIN BERGER

ANCHOR BOOKS

DOUBLEDAY

NEW YORK   LONDON   TORONTO   SYDNEY   AUCKLAND

An Anchor Book
PUBLISHED BY DOUBLEDAY
a division of Bantam Doubleday Dell Publishing Group, Inc.
666 Fifth Avenue, New York, New York 10103

ANCHOR BOOKS, DOUBLEDAY, and the portrayal of an anchor
are trademarks of Doubleday, a division of Bantam Doubleday
Dell Publishing Group, Inc.

Library of Congress Cataloging-in-Publication Data
Berger, Melvin.
   Guide to sonatas: music for one or two
   instruments / Melvin Berger.—1st Anchor
   Books ed.
      p.   cm.
   Discography. p.
   1. Sonata.   I. Title.
   ML1156.B46   1991   90-982
   784.18′3—dc20   CIP
                            MN

ISBN 0-385-41302-5

Contents

—CONTENTS—

Preface

SONATAS appear on practically every recital program. Piano recitals, violin and piano recitals, cello and piano recitals, and virtually every other solo and accompanied instrumental program contains at least one sonata. This book strives to help music lovers derive the maximum pleasure and satisfaction from their listening experiences by providing vital background information and helpful discussions and analyses of several hundred works in this form. The range of music covered stretches from Corelli to Copland, and includes all solo instruments and pairs of instruments.

The sonatas are arranged alphabetically by composer. For those composers who wrote only a limited number of sonatas, the works are considered in chronological order. For those who wrote a number of sonatas for particular instruments, the instruments are listed alphabetically and the individual sonatas follow in order of composition.

The amount of space devoted to each sonata varies. The major works—those that are published, recorded, and frequently performed—receive a full, in-depth discussion that establishes the historical and musical setting and presents the salient features of the music, including formal organization, musical content, and any extramusical associations. For compositions that are not central to the standard repertoire the discussion is, perforce, more limited.

Since this book aims to meet the needs of the general reader, as well as experienced concertgoers, record collectors, and performing musicians, technical terms are avoided wherever possible. Any unfamiliar words, along with brief explanations of such basic terms as *sonata* and *sonata form,* can be found in the Glossary.

A prominent sculptor was once asked how long it took him to complete a monumental sculpture. When he replied that it took sixteen months, the questioner expressed amazement, to which the sculptor responded, "More accurately, it took fifty-two years —and sixteen months!"

Likewise, while it took me somewhat over two years to write *Guide to Sonatas,* I brought to this labor of love many years of study, including three degrees in music; an active career as a viola solo recitalist (with appearances in New York, London, Washington, Philadelphia, and elsewhere), chamber musician, orchestral player, and teacher; considerable experience as a writer and lecturer on musical subjects; and a lifelong addiction to concertgoing.

Obviously, any attempt to provide a comprehensive guide to the vast sonata repertoire in a book of manageable length presents many problems of selection. To ensure that I treat all the works that readers are likely to encounter, without overloading the book with obscure, infrequently performed compositions, I exchanged ideas with many leading performers, studied stacks of concert programs, and consulted many record and publisher catalogs. I incorporated all of this information into my own thoughts to prepare what I hope is a complete, balanced selection of entries. While I may have omitted certain composers or compositions that others consider essential, I can only say that every decision was made as carefully and objectively as possible.

Guide to
SONATAS

Johann Sebastian Bach

Born March 21, 1685, in Eisenach, Germany
Died July 28, 1750, in Leipzig

AFTER being taught violin by his father and the keyboard instruments by an older brother, Bach served his musical apprenticeship in various minor German court positions. His first significant appointment was to the court of Duke Wilhelm Ernst in Weimar in 1708. Eight years later, because of growing disaffection with the duke and an offer to become Kapellmeister in the court of Prince Leopold of Anhalt-Cöthen at a much higher salary (400 thaler per year as opposed to 250 thaler in Weimar), Bach submitted his resignation. The duke refused to accept the request and when Bach pursued the matter, he had him thrown in jail for "too stubbornly" requesting to leave! Bach spent nearly a month behind bars, composing all the while, before the duke relented, releasing the composer from imprisonment and from service at the court.

Bach arrived in Cöthen at the end of 1717 and remained there until the spring of 1723 (when he accepted the final and most important position of his life, that of Cantor at Leipzig's St. Thomas church). It was here at Cöthen that Bach composed all of his sonatas. The chief incentive came from his employer, Prince Leopold, a true music lover who was proficient on the violin, viola da gamba, harpsichord, and was a gifted singer as well.

An added stimulus to Bach's involvement with purely instrumental composition was that the religious services at Cöthen were strictly Calvinist and therefore required little new, original music from the Kapellmeister. Consequently, between the musical interests of his patron and the limited demand for church music, Bach composed such outstanding works as the *Brandenburg Concertos,* the orchestral suites, Book I of *The Well-Tempered Clavier,* several concertos and, as we said, all of the sonatas during the six years he spent at Cöthen.

In Bach's day, the term *sonata* did not refer to the later, standard three- or four-movement composition, with a first movement in sonata-allegro form. In effect, Bach understood the sonata simply to be a "sound" piece—an instrumental work, as contrasted with a cantata—a sung, or vocal, composition.

With virtually no exceptions, all of his sonatas are of the type known as *sonata da chiesa* ("church sonata"). In general, they tend to be serious and somewhat abstract works, a reflection of their origin as music suitable for performance in religious services. The sonatas usually contain four separate sections, or movements, so named because each one moves at a different speed. Almost always, Bach's sonatas start with a slow movement that has some of the character of an introduction. It is followed by a fast, bright movement, often the most important one of the composition. The third movement, which is slow in tempo, is usually the most melodic, sometimes with a touch of pathos. And the fourth movement is the happy ending—a fast, joyous, high-spirited conclusion to the entire piece.

In addition to his sonatas, Bach composed a number of suites and partitas for one or two instruments. These works are closely akin to the *sonata da camera* ("chamber sonata") and differ from the *sonata da chiesa* type. The *sonata da camera,* as well as the suites and partitas, consist of a flexible sequence of movements in familiar dance rhythms and tend, in most cases, to be somewhat light in style.

The keyboard instrument in Bach's duo sonatas is commonly called either a clavier (literally "keyboard") or cembalo (from *clavicembalo,* Italian for "keyed dulcimer")—two terms that, in this context, mean harpsichord. While these duo sonatas were usually played on the piano during most of the nineteenth and twentieth centuries, in recent years, with the rise of the early-music movement and an increasing desire for authenticity in the performance of older music, Bach's keyboard parts are now frequently performed on the harpsichord. Hearing the music with the instrumentation that Bach intended gives a very different impression of these works and provides a much better blend between the two solo instruments.

The most accurate way of ordering Bach's compositions is by BWV number, which stands for *Bach Werke Verzeichnis,* a reference to Wolfgang Schmieder's thematic catalog of all of Bach's music.

Flute Sonatas

Bach wrote two sonatas for harpsichord and flute, the **Sonata for Cembalo and Flute in B minor, BWV 1030,** and **Sonata for Cembalo and Flute in A, BWV 1032.** (Sonatas BWV 1020 and 1031 are no longer believed to have been composed by Bach. Discussed below are the two sonatas for flute and *basso continuo* and the sonata for solo flute.)

Both of the sonatas for harpsichord and flute give mostly the effect of a trio with three independent voices—flute, right hand of the harpsichord, and left hand of the harpsichord—each voice comprised of single notes. Only rarely does the harpsichord stray from this linear texture and play a more chordal part.

The Bach biographer Philipp Spitta calls the B minor sonata "the finest flute sonata in existence." Composed originally in the key of G minor around the year 1720, Bach transposed it to its present key in the 1730s to better suit the flute's range. Grand and expansive in conception, the first movement is contrapuntal and polyphonic in texture throughout. The Largo e dolce (second movement), in contrast to the first movement, maintains a predominantly homophonic texture, with arpeggiated chords in the harpsichord supporting the lyrical flute line. The finale falls into two distinct, separate parts, first a three-voice fugue and then a busy, bustling section that is a variation on the fugue theme.

The A major sonata lacks some fifty measures from its first movement owing to a most unfortunate set of circumstances. When Bach wrote out the score for his Concerto for Two Claviers, three music staves were left blank at the bottom of each page. The parsimonious composer decided to squeeze the flute sonata onto those staves to save music paper. Sometime later the bottoms of pages 9 through 14 of the two claviers concerto were cut off, resulting in the present gap. Although the first movement includes only the first sixty-two and last two measures, the sonata is such an excellent work that it is often played with movements two and three only, or with a reconstruction of the absent section. A gentle, bittersweet mood is created in the slow second movement, with the flute singing its lovely melody and the harpsichord lending support with its closely related countermelody. The bright and rollicking Allegro third movement moves along mostly in canonic imitation.

The **Sonata for Flute Solo in A minor, BWV 1013**, was also almost lost because of Bach's penny-pinching ways. Some years ago, when studying the manuscript of the composer's solo violin sonatas, musicologist Karl Straube found this hitherto unknown sonata crowded onto the blank last page of those works! Since it is in Bach's hand and style, it is now commonly accepted as authentic.

Two questions, though, continue to bedevil Bach scholars when it comes to this piece: When composing for a wind instrument, in which the player needs time to breathe, why did Bach write a first movement with but one chance to catch a breath in the entire movement? And why did he call it a sonata, since its four dancelike movements make it much more like a suite? Although there are no easy answers, one can suggest that Bach may have been thinking more of a violin than a flute when he was writing the first movement, and that it is indeed a sonata, but of the sonata da camera type, rather than the usual sonata da chiesa.

Even though Bach calls the first movement an Allemande (a dance in the German style), its ceaseless flow of equal sixteenth notes prevents easy identification based on its rhythmic pattern. The movement is a good test of the performer's skill in sneaking in quick gulps of air without interfering with the ongoing rush of notes.

The Corrente ("running" in Italian) feels much more comfortable from the viewpoint of breath control. It is also happier, more ingratiating, and more appealing in comparison with the preceding movement.

Bach invests the Sarabande—an old dance, probably Spanish in origin and typically in slow, stately triple meter—with a great deal of emotional content. Keeping the flute low in its register imbues it with a special poignancy, and the comparatively simple, slow-moving melodic line gives flutists the opportunity to add improvisatory embellishments.

The scintillating Bourrée anglaise provides a spirited, captivating finish to the sonata.

The **Sonata for Flute and Basso Continuo in E minor, BWV 1034,** and **Sonata for Flute and Basso Continuo in E, BWV 1035,** are both authentic compositions by Bach; a third such sonata, BWV 1033, is now believed spurious. These works for flute are composed in a style of writing known as *basso continuo*—figured bass or thoroughbass. The original manuscript showed only the flute line and a bass line for the harpsichord, plus various numbers and symbols under the harpsichord notes. In performance the bass line is played by the left hand of the harpsichordist as well as by a viola da gamba player. And the numbers tell the keyboard player what chords and harmonies to build on the bass notes.

In a process known as realizing the basso continuo, the keyboard performers have much latitude in arranging the chords and adding melodies and ornaments to the basic harmonies indicated by the composer. Since few keyboard players today have the skills to realize a basso continuo on the spot, as did the players in Bach's time, most modern editions contain a printed part in which this figured bass is completely written out.

Both sonatas, E minor and E major, follow the same basic plan. The slow first movement has the flute playing a cantilena (smooth, melodious) line over chords in the harpsichord, with a bass melody in the left hand of the harpsichord and the viola da gamba. A bright, sprightly movement with dancelike rhythms follows. Languid in tempo, the third movement is expressive, much like an arioso or song. The finale resembles the second movement in its fast tempo and lively mood.

The fact that so many handwritten copies of the E minor flute sonata survive from Bach's day testifies to its great popularity when it first appeared. On the other hand, the E major sonata exists today only because Bach gave a copy of the work to King Frederick the Great and it was later found in the king's library.

Viola da Gamba (Cello or Viola) Sonatas

Bach wrote three sonatas for the most popular member of the viol family of string instruments, the viola da gamba, a six-string fretted instrument, held between the knees somewhat like a cello, which produces a soft, delicate tone. Since only a limited number of early music specialists play the viola da gamba today, the sonatas are much more frequently performed in transcriptions for either cello or viola.

The **Sonata for Clavier and Viola da Gamba No. 1 in G, BWV 1027,** first appeared around 1720 as a sonata for two flutes (BWV 1039), but Bach transcribed it for the present combination of instruments in the 1730s. The sonata still maintains, though, the same three voices of the original—the gamba and right hand of the harpsichord playing the two flute parts, and the left hand of the harpsichord playing the bass line.

With the opening Adagio, Bach immediately establishes the warm, welcoming tone that pervades the entire sonata. Graceful melodic phrases gently pass in imitation from gamba to harpsichord and from hand to hand on the harpsichord.

Although not very fast, the second movement has a momentum that propels it forward while the composer spins an intricate web of imitative counterpoint around the tune, which is first presented by the right hand of the harpsichord.

Imitation is again the rule in the third movement as the long arching melody comes first in the right hand of the harpsichord with the gamba two beats behind and then with the string instrument taking the lead.

Spiced with a sprinking of syncopations, the Allegro moderato creates a three-voice fugue based on a subject introduced by the harpsichordist's right hand.

The least known of the three sonatas, the **Sonata for Clavier and Viola da Gamba No. 2 in D, BWV 1028,** is a tight compact work in which the treatment is almost exclusively imitative counterpoint.

The extremely short and highly emotional opening Adagio leads directly into the much more substantial Allegro, and gives the impression of being more an introduction than an independent first movement.

Although fast in tempo, the second movement lacks some of the snap and energy of a more typical Bach Allegro. The initial rhythmic pattern, presented in both the gamba and the harpsichord right hand, runs throughout the entire movement, either in its original form or in variation.

Returning to the expressivity of the opening movement, the Andante is built on an especially beautiful extended melodic line, which passes from voice to voice as the movement progresses.

Motoric and propulsive in character, the finale is infused with attractive dance-rhythm patterns, which make this the most accessible movement of the sonata.

With the **Sonata for Clavier and Viola da Gamba No. 3 in B flat, BWV 1029,** Bach seems to enter a new and even greater realm of creativity. In Spitta's words, it is "a work of the highest beauty and the most striking originality." Containing only three instead of the usual four movements, the sonata opens with a Vivace that surges ahead with an elemental, almost ferocious, verve and dash. Perhaps the most striking moment occurs near the end of the movement when all three voices, which had been moving along with great contrapuntal independence and freedom, suddenly combine in a powerful unison statement of the theme.

An almost religious hush pervades the slow movement, the Adagio, as all three voices sing their melodic lines with devotional fervor.

The start of the concluding Allegro, with the gamba giving out a vigorous, dancelike theme, leads one to expect the rest of the movement to be devoted to a working out of that subject. Instead Bach introduces a sharply contrasting melody that is much more cantabile and lyrical in articulation. The remainder of the movement treats both themes, often with a brilliance and virtuosity not encountered in the other gamba sonatas.

Violin Sonatas

Bach wrote six sonatas for harpsichord and violin, with the keyboard part completely written out, rather than just a bass line, as in the sonatas for one instrument and basso continuo. Since the violin plays a single melody line and each hand of the harpsichord, for the most part, plays single notes, the resultant texture resembles that of a trio.

The **Sonata for Clavier and Violin No. 1 in B minor, BWV 1014,** can be deemed an overall serious work. The slow first movement sounds mournful with the downward-moving sighs in the right hand, the highly expressive reiterated figure in the left hand, and the slow-moving melancholy melody in the violin.

The faster Allegro begins as a three-voice fugue, continues with a development of the fugue subject, and ends with a literal repeat of the opening fugue.

The violin plays a melody of luminous beauty in the third movement, with a "walking" bass in the left hand of the harpsichord part and a delicate tracery in the right hand.

A hammered, repeated note distinguishes the theme of the finale, which maintains a fugal and contrapuntal texture throughout.

The restrained and quiet opening movement of the **Sonata for Clavier and Violin No. 2 in A, BWV 1015,** furnishes a kind of foil to the bravura Allegro assai that follows. Hearing the brilliant, virtuosic fugal writing of the second movement makes one appreciate Bach's well-realized intention to start with the modest beginning in order to heighten, by contrast, the impact of this concertante movement.

The following slow movement is a perfect canon; the violin states the tender, expressive melody, which the right hand of the harpsichord imitates one measure later.

The Presto is light in character and has an attractive marchlike rhythmic swing.

The harpsichord presents the melody in short, separate

phrases in the first movement of the **Sonata for Clavier and Violin No. 3 in E, BWV 1016,** while the violin soars freely above.

Jazzy and jocund, the second movement theme appears first in the harpsichord and is then taken up by the violin. After a delightful development of the tune it comes once more, this time played by the violin followed by the harpsichord.

The tender, moving Adagio ma non tanto—the climactic movement of the sonata—shows some resemblance to the chaconne, an ancient form in which a short phrase, usually in the bass, is repeated over and over again under ever-changing, continuous variations.

Highly rhythmic and very busy, the Allegro provides a joyous, playful conclusion to the sonata.

The **Sonata for Clavier and Violin No. 4 in C minor, BWV 1017,** starts with a lengthy, sectional Siciliano that, instead of being typically idyllic and pastoral, sounds rather dark and grieving.

A big, rich fast movement comes next; its first section presents the contrapuntal thematic material, which is varied and developed in the second section and returned, though not literally, in the third section, with a concluding coda.

Calm and peaceful, the Adagio consists basically of an alternately loud and soft expansion and variation of the opening melody.

Using a vigorous, dancelike melody, the final Allegro resembles a three-voice fugue in structure.

In the opening Largo of the **Sonata for Clavier and Violin No. 5 in F minor, BWV 1018,** Bach adds another line to the usual two in the harpsichord and creates a particularly rich four-voice texture; melodically it is based on the mournful melody from his motet *Komm, Jesu, komm.*

Sharply contrasting with the plaintive solemnity of the first movement is the vital, driving fugal Allegro that follows.

In the slow movement, the violin, playing two notes simultaneously (called double stops), spins a simple, though profound and dreamlike melody, while the two hands of the harpsichord part continue their ongoing dialogue.

The concluding Vivace sparkles with syncopations and brilliant writing for the two instruments.

The **Sonata for Clavier and Violin No. 6 in G, BWV 1019,** appears in two earlier versions. The first started with a fast movement, followed by three slow movements, and ended with a repetition of the first. The second version included movements for harpsichord alone and for violin alone. The final version begins with the same opening movement as before—a flashy, exciting display for both instruments. Retained also from the original, the Largo features a beautifully grave melody. Bach supplied a completely new, extended third movement, which turned out to be a rich, full-voiced solo for the harpsichord. One hears both passion and yearning in the following Adagio with its highly chromatic melody. The sonata ends with an irresistible burst of energy in the fifth movement.

Some editions of Bach's works for solo violin incorrectly list the contents as six sonatas, instead of three sonatas and three partitas. And it is these three true sonatas that are among the most magnificent and monumental musical creations of all time. That Bach took on himself the audacious challenge of writing music with as many as four separate voices for the essentially single-voice violin is an act of incredible arrogance; that he succeeds so splendidly is little short of miraculous!

Working in his favor was the construction of violins in the early eighteenth century; the top of the violin bridge—the upright support for the strings that stands on the belly of the violin —was flatter than today's bridge and the bow hairs were looser. (The mechanical screw to tighten the hairs had been invented, but it was slow in being accepted.) Consequently, it was somewhat easier, although never completely comfortable, to play on three or four strings simultaneously, as Bach required in these sonatas.

Modern violinists, playing instruments with highly arched bridges and tighter bows, are forced to sound the individual notes of the three- and four-note chords sequentially, rather than simultaneously. Because they are not able to keep all the notes sounding, they must drop some notes in order to sustain others. Some critics complain that, even in the hands of the most able violinists, a certain harshness results from the players' efforts to create musical effects that can only be suggested as a consequence of the technical limitations of modern instruments.

How then do violinists manage to play multivoice music on the single-voice violin? For playing two notes, the performer merely rests the bow on two strings and plays both notes simultaneously; the only limitation is that the notes be playable on adjacent strings and that both fall within the grasp of the four fingers. To play three- or four-note chords requires a bit of legerdemain, a sort of musical *trompe l'oreille.* The violinist rolls the bow across the strings and gets as close to sounding all the notes simultaneously as possible, allowing some notes to continue to ring while moving on to others. Listeners are expected to supply, in their mind's ear, the notes and lines of melody that must occasionally be omitted.

Each of the three peerless sonatas—the **Sonata for Violin Solo in G minor, BWV 1001; Sonata for Violin Solo in A minor, BWV 1003;** and **Sonata for Violin Solo in C, BWV 1005**—has many special features that distinguish it from the others. Yet all follow the same basic organizational scheme and therefore can be discussed as a single, unified group.

All three sonatas contain four movements. Movements one, two, and four are in the same key; the third movement is in a different key.

Movement one: Slow tempo; solemn and serious in character; much use of three- and four-note chords.

Movement two: Fast tempo; called a fugue, but more accurately described as a contrapuntal movement with many extended fugal passages in which the same melody occurs at different times starting on different notes; a forceful and fiery movement that often serves as the sonata's musical capstone.

Movement three: Slow tempo; point of repose after the tension and agitation of the fugue; lyrical style, with the chords functioning more as accompaniment than as independent voices.

Movement four: Fast tempo; single line throughout; lively and spirited, with a perpetual motion–like flow of rapid notes, which adds a touch of virtuosity; the lightest movement from the viewpoint of musical substance.

Samuel Barber

Born March 9, 1910, in West Chester, Pennsylvania
Died January 23, 1981, in New York City

WHEN Samuel Barber was about eight years old, growing more and more interested in piano studies and making his first efforts at composing, his parents urged him to spend more time playing ball with friends. He responded with a note to his mother that said in part, "I was not meant to be an athelet. I was meant to be a composer. And will be, I'm sure."

A composer Barber did become—and rather quickly, too. By age twenty-one he had written *Dover Beach* for voice and string quartet, and *Overture to The School for Scandal,* which were premiered by Rose Bampton and the New York String Quartet, and the Philadelphia Orchestra, respectively.

In 1932 Barber composed his **Sonata for Cello and Piano, Op. 6.** This was the last work completed under the guidance of Rosario Scalero, his composition teacher at the Curtis Institute, and the dedicatee of the sonata. A richly imaginative work characterized by its strength, vitality, and passion, it led critics to designate Barber a Neoromantic, a composer who realizes in twentieth-century terms the musical ideals of the nineteenth century, the so-called Romantic period.

The sonata is cast in three movements. Starting at the very beginning with the principal theme of the first movement, a soaring, upward-reaching cello melody, one can hear the distinguishing characteristics of Barber's style—the primacy of melody, the vocal quality of every note and musical gesture, and the fervor that burns with great intensity throughout, with the occasional quiet moments providing the time and relaxation needed to prepare for the next ardent climax. The cello carries most of the melodic burden in the movement, singing its generous outpouring of melody with only minimal contribution from the piano.

The second movement is really two movements in one. It begins slowly, leading to the expectation that it will be a typical slow movement. But then Barber interrupts with a fast, scherzolike interlude, a reference to the usual third movement. And he concludes with the deliberate tempo and character of the opening, thus effectively achieving a synthesis of both the slow movement and scherzo.

Traditionally, the final movement of a sonata is a brilliant, happy conclusion to all that has gone before. While there are some moments of virtuosic writing, Barber's finale avoids flash and glitter. It is serious and weighty in demeanor, moderate in tempo, and formally rather fragmented and sectional. The composer's goal seems more to engender a strong emotional response than to dazzle or entertain.

Barber composed his **Piano Sonata, Op. 26,** in 1949, seventeen years after the cello sonata. He wrote it on a commission from the popular Broadway musical writers Irving Berlin and Richard Rodgers through the League of Composers.

While still maintaining some allegiance to the music of the past, the extremely emotional piano sonata goes far beyond the cello sonata in its use of twentieth-century compositional techniques. Highly dissonant and chromatic, the work makes some use of twelve-tone technique, a compositional system devised by Arnold Schoenberg in the 1920s. Stated simply, the technique requires that some arrangement of all twelve notes of the chromatic scale, called a tone row, be heard before any note can be repeated. Barber adapted the twelve-tone system rather freely, though; he used not one row, but several, and did not hesitate to violate the rules of twelve-tone composition when it suited his musical purpose.

The fearsomely difficult piano writing requires extraordinary technical skill on the part of the interpreter. For a number of years, this burden limited performances of the work. In addition to the problem of mastering the piece's intricacies and playing it well, there was the risk of being compared with the brilliant Vladimir Horowitz, who made the sonata a central part of his repertoire. In recent years, though, pianists have become more venturesome and the work has assumed its rightful place on recital programs.

The first movement bursts forth with an angry, dissonant, highly rhythmic theme. Although there are some quiet moments, the tension and uncompromising drive are felt throughout, reaching a climax at the return of the opening melody.

The scherzo that follows releases some of the built-up intensity and tension. Motoric in rhythm and confined mostly to the piano's upper register, the movement contains a middle section that provides a delightful, though brief, waltzlike interlude.

Barber's biographer, Nathan Broder, calls the Adagio mesto "the most tragic of all of Barber's slow movements." It is here that Barber makes the greatest use of the twelve-tone row. Many listeners, however, find that they are more moved by the anguish expressed in the music than they are aware of the technical devices used by the composer.

The fugal finale, a splendid exercise in contrapuntal imitation, sparkles with rhythmic vitality. This fiendishly difficult movement makes some short references to Gershwin-like turns of melody before returning to the original propulsive energy and hurtling on to the ending.

Béla Bartók

Born March 25, 1881, in Nagyszentmiklós, Hungary
Died September 26, 1945, in New York City

THE pivotal factor in Bartók's musical development was his discovery, during the summer of 1904, of the rich Hungarian peasant music heritage—not Gypsy music or the romanticized folk melodies offered by Liszt and Brahms, but the pure, authentic, national folk music of Hungary. Bartók devoted so many years to collecting and studying this material that it became an integral part of his musical vocabulary. He did not have to quote folksongs; every phrase he wrote was infused with ethnic melodies and rhythms.

By the early 1920s, however, Bartók was losing some of his enthusiasm for composing music that was rooted exclusively in folk music. In addition, the innovative compositions of Arnold Schoenberg and Igor Stravinsky were in the air, and Bartók found himself coming under their stylistic influence. For example, in Bartók's music from this period one can hear his adaptation of Schoenberg's twelve-tone method of composition and of Stravinsky's use of brief motifs that are repeated and varied in a harsh, driving way.

Troubled by the lessening role of folk elements in his serious compositions and the strong influence of the two seminal composers, Bartók began to suffer feelings of doubt and insecurity. This unsettled condition was exacerbated by the disordered conditions in Hungary following World War I and the imminent breakup of his marriage, which ended in divorce in August 1923.

The representative works from this turbulent time are the closely related **First Sonata for Violin and Piano** and **Second Sonata for Violin and Piano**. As the Bartók biographer Serge Moreux put it, the sonatas are "linked to each other as night and day." They followed each other in short order; the first was composed from October to December 1921, the second from July to November 1922. Both were dedicated to violinist Jelly d'Arányi, who gave the premieres in London with the composer at the piano. The sonatas are less "Bartókian" than almost any of his mature works, and are marked more by the influence of Schoenberg and Stravinsky than by the presence of indigenous folk elements.

The music is "difficult" in that the rhythms are in continuous flux, with shifting meters and tempi; the melodies are unvocal, hard to identify, and often characterized by giant leaps within the melodic line; and the harmonies are strange and dissonant, seemingly more concerned with individual sonorities than with harmonic progressions. The writing gives most of the melodic burden to the violin, with the piano frequently furnishing a percussive harmonic underpinning; there is almost no sharing or interchange of melodic material between the two instruments.

The First Violin Sonata presents the more uncompromising and demanding aspects. Bartók later confessed that he liked it less than the Second Sonata and was particularly dissatisfied with the first movement—an intense, emotional musical maelstrom, rife with shrieks and sobs, with even the more tranquil moments robbed of any relaxed feelings because of the searing dissonances.

A strongly lyrical contrasting movement follows; some sections are written in a flexible, irregular rhythm known as *parlando-rubato,* in which the music imitates the free rhythms and inflections of human speech. The melodic line adheres to the principles of Schoenberg's twelve-tone method, in which all 12 notes of the chromatic scale are sounded before any are repeated.

The concluding Allegro, perhaps the most accessible movement, is a sort of perpetual motion, based on fragments of energetic Magyar dance rhythms. The wildness and great spirit of this bravura movement, which drives through to a brilliant end-ing, are reminiscent of the young Stravinsky.

The Second Violin Sonata, a much more concentrated, com-pact work, lasts little more than half as long as the first sonata, and is in two rather than three movements. The first movement emerges languorous and deliberate, with much use made of the speechlike *parlando-rubato* amid a generally gentle and melan-cholic air. Two special devices that Bartók employs here to great effect are *glissando*—sliding from one pitch to the next—and har-monics—touching the string lightly with a finger to produce a high-pitched whistling tone instead of a solid note.

Following without pause, the second movement starts with a few notes of introduction in the piano before the violin enters *pizzicato* (plucking the strings) softly and slowly. Gradually, as the movement progresses, the tempo and the energy level in-crease and we are soon swept along in the wild abandon of a Hungarian fiddle dance. Bartók interrupts the proceedings near the end for a slow reminder of the sonata's opening theme be-fore ending the work quietly and wistfully.

After composing the two violin sonatas and his orchestral Dance Suite in 1923, Bartók wrote no major works until 1926, when he devoted the entire year to producing music for piano, notably the Piano Sonata, the suite *Out of Doors,* and the First Piano Concerto. Since Bartók had a very active career as a per-forming virtuoso pianist, he composed these for his own use, the sonata to be the major work at his solo recitals and the concerto to serve the same purpose in his engagements with orchestra.

In the **Sonata for Piano** Bartók's affinity for Hungarian folk music becomes tempered by other influences. "In my youth," he said, "Bach and Mozart were not my ideals of the beautiful, but rather Beethoven. During the last few years, I have been occu-pied with pre-Bach music." On another occasion he said, "As a man grows more mature, it seems that he has a greater longing to be more economical with his means, in order to achieve sim-plicity." As a result, his music took on a spareness and objectiv-ity, which can also be heard in the music being written during those same years by such Neoclassical composers as Stravinsky and Hindemith.

The piano writing in the sonata may be described as motoric—mechanical and relentless—percussive, and highly dissonant. Bartók makes frequent use of tone clusters, playing two or more adjacent notes simultaneously, more for their effect as discordant noise than for harmonic or melodic purposes. All the themes are confined to a narrow compass of notes and many feature a good number of repeated notes.

Following the outline of traditional sonata-allegro form, the first movement hurtles forward with great propulsive force. The hammerlike notes create a highly charged, exciting tonal ambiance, and the rhythmic drive never slackens, gaining even more speed at the very end.

Although austere and stark in sound, the second movement projects a certain eloquence and expressivity. As in the first movement, one is conscious of the many repeated notes underlying the lyrical fragments of melody.

The final movement bursts out in joyous radiance. Using folklike themes, Bartók fills the air with happiness and merriment, providing a positive, affirmative conclusion to the entire sonata.

No composer can write a sonata for an unaccompanied string instrument without drawing heavily on the Bach sonatas for solo violin—and Bartók is no exception. His **Sonata for Solo Violin**, which is Baroque in framework, includes such favorite forms as the chaconne and fugue, but is strictly Bartókian in its basic approach to the instrument.

It was on a 1943 commission from violinist Yehudi Menuhin, long a champion of Bartók's music, that the composer wrote the sonata. Bartók had lived in the United States since October 1940, after he was forced to flee his beloved Hungary, and worked on the music during February and March 1944 in Asheville, North Carolina. At this point in his career he was recovering from hospitalization for the treatment of leukemia, a disease that was to take his life eighteen months later.

The Bartók biographer György Kroó notes four major influences in this solo violin sonata: the obvious connection with Bach and the Baroque sonata; the folklike quality that pervades the music; Bartók's preference for the formal structures favored by Beethoven; and finally the streak of Romanticism that is most easily heard in his very early works.

The first movement of the fiendishly difficult sonata is marked Tempo di ciaconna, "tempo of a chaconne," a popular Baroque form characterized by continuous variation on a short snatch of melody, usually in triple time (three beats to a measure) and moving in a slow, stately tempo. True to the title, Bartók adopted a typical chaconne rhythm, but virtually ignored the variation aspect in favor of organizing the movement along the lines of a traditional sonata-allegro, with an exposition, development, and recapitulation.

The Fuga that follows begins as a conventional fugue, with the same laconic theme—growing from a two-note motif, but slightly changed in each appearance—passing in imitation through four separate voices, a feat of musical magic, considering that only the solo violin is available. In time, though, Bartók allows the music to develop into a rather free fantasy on the fugal subject.

Considered by some to be the finest movement of the sonata, the following Melodia is cast in three parts. The first presents an extended melody of warm, tender beauty. The contrasting middle section, what Bartók called his "night music," evokes the distant sounds of nature—a dimly heard bird song, the murmuring of wind through the trees. The composer creates these effects by having the violin play double stops (two notes at once), along with many trills (the rapid alternation of two adjacent notes). He then brings back the first part, but so changed—two octaves higher and much embellished—that it may well take a few hearings to become aware of its relationship with the opening.

The main theme of the Presto is a rushing, swirling flow of notes. In the original manuscript, Bartók incorporated a number of quarter tones, notes that come between the usual half steps of Western music, and that sound out of tune to our ears. For some unknown reason, though, the published version changes these quarter tones to half steps and it is frequently performed that way. The movement is organized as a rondo, with the scurrying opening returning two more times, its appearances separated by interludes that seem to be derived from folksong sources.

Ludwig van Beethoven

Born December 16, 1770, in Bonn
Died March 26, 1827, in Vienna

PERHAPS Leonard Bernstein provided the pithiest definition of Beethoven's genius when he wrote that Beethoven had "the inexplicable ability to know what the next note has to be." This sense of inevitability, of "rightness," in his music puts Beethoven on a par with the greatest artistic creators of all time, the Shakespeares, Rembrandts, Michelangelos, and others of that tiny company.

Beethoven brought to maturity the most important forms of Classical instrumental music—the symphony, string quartet, solo concerto, and sonata. In so doing he liberated music from its eighteenth-century restrictions and restraints, and established a style and a means of expression that have influenced, to greater or lesser degree, every composer who has followed.

Born in Bonn, at that time a small, provincial town, Beethoven's first exposure to music was through his father, a dissolute, untalented court musician. By age twenty-one, Beethoven had settled in Vienna, where he completed his studies with Haydn and won a reputation both as pianist and composer. Some seven years later, though, he began to realize that he was losing his hearing. For the remaining three decades of his life, even while struggling with ever worsening deafness, ill health, and innumerable personal, family, and financial crises, he was able to produce some of the greatest works of music the world knows.

As a young man, Beethoven was well aware of the winds of social, political, and economic change blowing through Europe, culminating in the French Revolution of 1789. Although poorly educated in subjects outside music, Beethoven read widely and believed passionately in the basic principle of the revolution— the right of all people to live in freedom and dignity, protected from the egregious greed and power of the nobles. As part of the process of democratization taking place during his lifetime, the focus of music was shifting away from churches and the palaces of the aristocracy to the concert halls of the bourgeoisie. In giving shape and substance to this new music, Beethoven helped change the role of the composer from craftsman—who provided music to satisfy his patron's demands, to creative artist—who composed in response to his own inner needs and urges.

Beethoven turned out three groups of sonatas—five for cello, thirty-two for piano, and ten for violin. These sonatas, virtually without exception, have assumed central positions in today's recital repertoire.

Cello Sonatas

Beethoven's five cello sonatas, although few in number as compared to his works for the piano or violin, effectively cover the three major creative periods of his life. The two works in Op. 5, the single Op. 69, and the two Op. 102 sonatas provide excellent representative examples of his first, middle, and final periods, respectively.

The **Sonata for Piano and Cello No. 1 in F, Op. 5, No. 1**, and **Sonata for Piano and Cello No. 2 in G minor, Op. 5, No. 2**, were written just before or during Beethoven's trip to Berlin early in 1796. The composer dedicated them to Friedrich Wilhelm II, King of Prussia, who was an accomplished amateur cellist. The leading cello player in the king's orchestra, Jean-Louis Duport, gave the premiere at the royal court in Berlin with Beethoven at the piano. In appreciation, the king presented the delighted Beethoven with a gold snuffbox stuffed with one hundred louis d'or. Beethoven later boasted that "it was not an ordinary snuffbox, but one that might customarily have been given to an ambassador." (The coins were worth over five hundred dollars at the time; but that amount must be multiplied many times over to determine today's equivalent value.)

While many of his early sonatas were composed in the shadow of comparable works by Haydn or Mozart, Beethoven had no precedents for his cello sonatas, since neither older composer had ever essayed that particular combination. In part this can be attributed to the cello's rather late liberation from its role of doubling the bass line of the keyboard instrument in the Baroque basso continuo compositional style. Even in the Op. 5 sonatas one senses some vestigial remains of the cello in this role, that the pieces are more keyboard sonatas with an added cello part, rather than music of two equal partners. Beethoven's wording—sonatas for *piano and cello*—also reminds us that the keyboard sonata had been dominant throughout the eighteenth century, and duo sonatas therefore tended to relegate the second instrument to a subsidiary, accompanying role. And it is likely that Beethoven conceived many of the melodic figures at the keyboard, which would also make him incline to give the piano a more important role than the cello.

Beethoven organizes the two sonatas similarly: they both contain only two movements. The first movements started with a long, slow melodic introduction; the fast sections that follow without pause are in traditional sonata-allegro outline. And the second movements take the form of a rondo, with a light vivacious character and ingenuous charm.

How to explain this unorthodox structure? Perhaps Beethoven chose the slow/fast opening movement in imitation of the Baroque sonatas, which usually start with two such movements and are traditionally played with little or no break between them. Or he may have been concerned about the difficulty of sustaining musical interest in a full-length slow movement with a tenor-voiced instrument. On the other hand, it may simply have been Beethoven's way of immediately establishing the rich, sonorous cello sound. It is difficult to know Beethoven's precise motives, but one thing is sure. The sonatas have the great appeal, the youthful enthusiasm, virility, freshness of writing and sure confidence of an immensely talented and able twenty-six-year-old composer.

The **Sonata for Piano and Cello No. 3 in A, Op.** 69, with its interesting blend of graceful buoyancy and profound depth, falls midway between the Op. 5 sonatas and those of Op. 102 in both time and character. One of the most striking features of Op. 69 is its much more important and fully realized cello part as compared with the Op. 5 sonatas.

Composed in 1807 and 1808, the Op. 69 sonata is dedicated to Baron Ignaz von Gleichenstein, a young amateur cellist and Beethoven's best friend for several years. Gleichenstein was probably chosen for the dedication because he handled much of Beethoven's business affairs and helped to arrange the pensions from the several nobles who helped to support the composer.

Beethoven's words, written in Latin on the manuscript, "Amid tears and sorrow," have led to speculation about possible extramusical associations. One possible reference has to do with the fact that Gleichenstein and Beethoven were courting the two Malfatti sisters at the time the piece was written. Gleichenstein's suit was successful; Beethoven's failed. Since the sonata's restrained emotional content can hardly be described as being between "tears and sorrow," many believe Beethoven's comment refers to his despair over being rejected in love.

The theme that the unaccompanied cello presents to open the sonata has been described by some as a "perfect" melody; it is calm, noble, and warm, although not without a certain agitated and active quality. The imaginative working-out of this melody, the simple triadic and scalar second theme, and the richly romantic concluding theme, follow the dictates of traditional sonata-allegro form, including a triumphant unison statement of the main theme before the ending.

The lighthearted and rhythmically piquant Scherzo creates the illusion of a melody one beat out of phase. The first section occurs three times—before, between, and after the two appearances of the quiet, pensive trio, with its double stops (two notes at the same time) in the cello part.

At the conclusion of the Scherzo the piano starts a poised, deliberate melody that suggests the beginning of a proper slow movement, perhaps a theme and variations. But after the cello statement of the same melody, the music hesitates, and it becomes clear that this is nothing more than an introduction to the fast finale. Beethoven sets off on a gay, sparkling romp, a rondo, with a main subject that is as beautifully crafted as the first-movement theme. With but a few brief interruptions, the high-spirited music bubbles through to a brilliant conclusion.

The **Sonata for Piano and Cello No. 4 in C, Op. 102, No. 1,** and **Sonata for Piano and Cello No. 5 in D, Op. 102, No. 2,** are among those works that signal Beethoven's entry into his final creative period. At this point he was completely deaf and had turned away from the heroic style and virtuosic perspective that had informed so many of his earlier compositions. His attention was now completely focused on creating music on the most exalted, spiritual plane, unimpeded by such earthly concerns as the instrument's traditionally accepted technical limitations or the usual canons of musical composition. In his singleminded quest for pure musical expression he disregarded all that was trivial or superficial. Curiously enough, scholars note that even Beethoven's handwriting changed as he came into this new phase!

Beethoven composed the Op. 102 sonatas during the summer of 1815, his only major works in that year. He dedicated them to Countess Marie von Erdödy, in whose Vienna home he had lodgings. The premiere was probably given there by Beethoven's friend, the cellist Joseph Linke, who also taught the countess's children.

The C major sonata, the shortest of the five works for cello, is subtitled "Free Sonata," a reference to the unusual organization of the work into two symmetrical movements—both with slow introductions before much longer fast sections. The opening Andante starts with a gentle, tender songlike theme, one that ideally and most suitably projects the special beauty of the cello's tone. The introduction leads directly into the vigorous Allegro vivace, with its highly rhythmic, striding main theme.

A short, slow Adagio, reminiscent of an operatic recitative, opens the last movement. But before proceeding to the fast section, Beethoven brings back a brief reminder of the beginning Andante. Then, without pause, the fast, cheerful final movement emerges and races along gaily, with but a few characteristic inter-ruptions.

Not only does Beethoven eliminate all introductions in his D major sonata, but he detonates a musical explosion as the bold, dramatic first theme erupts at the very beginning with startling force. The composer then goes on to fashion a movement of brilliant tonal colors, great melodic variety, and continuous har-monic interest.

The profound and deeply moving Adagio constitutes the only full, true slow movement in all the cello sonatas. Although writ-ten quite sparely and imbued with a somewhat remote, distant quality, the music conveys a sublime, introspective, emotional richness. In this movement we hear the transcendental Beetho-ven penetrating a realm of musical expression that few have ever approached and almost none have conquered.

After providing the peak experience of the Adagio, Beetho-ven's inspiration does not flag as he goes on to finish the sonata with an amazing fugato. In this highly contrapuntal movement, one melody—somewhat ungainly in shape and extremely un-grateful to play—interweaves between the two instruments in an extremely intricate pattern of statements, counterstatements, imi-tations, countermelodies, inversions, and all the other poly-phonic devices that Beethoven's fertile imagination can conjure up. This movement presents the earliest manifestation of Bee-thoven's obsession with fugues (as witness the "Hammer-klavier" piano sonata and the *Grosse Fuge* for string quartet) that distinguished the final compositional epoch of his life.

Piano Sonatas

Bach's *Well-Tempered Clavier* has been dubbed the Old Testament of piano music and the thirty-two sonatas of Beethoven the New Testament. The latter works join Bach's masterpieces on the loft-iest heights of the solo piano repertoire—if not of all instrumen-tal music. Composed as they were throughout his life, the sona-tas trace Beethoven's growth and development as a composer and human being, even as they illuminate the transition in music history from the Classical to the Romantic periods.

When Beethoven arrived in Vienna at age twenty-one he started composition studies with Haydn—an experience that did little to advance Beethoven's skills. The mix of world-renowned composer just returned from great triumphs in London and the headstrong, sublimely confident Beethoven was not a happy one and the relationship between the two men was strained and difficult.

Nevertheless, Beethoven saw fit to dedicate his first piano sonatas—the set of three that make up his Op. 2—to Haydn. Composed in 1795 and 1796, the works were written after Beethoven had already completed three piano sonatas and two sonatinas that he did not submit for publication. The simple words on the manuscript, "To Joseph Haydn, Doctor of Music," express respect—but much less affection than, for example, Mozart's inscription on his "Haydn" string quartets to his "most celebrated and very dear friend." The restrained language of the dedication may also have something to do with Haydn's cooler response to Beethoven in comparison to his feelings for Mozart, whom Haydn called "the greatest composer known to me." In fact, Haydn often referred to Beethoven only half jokingly as the "Grand Mogul."

The **Piano Sonata No. 1 in F minor, Op. 2, No. 1,** opens with the so-called Mannheim rocket, a device much favored by late eighteenth-century composers in which a brilliant, rapidly rising figure arrests everyone's attention at the beginning of a piece. The ascending rocket, which in this case includes a few notes of descent, is repeated, extended, and rent with a veritable explosion of sound to make up the first subject. With barely any transition, the subsidiary theme follows, quiet and subdued and generally downward in melodic direction. Both themes are carefully considered in the brief development section and are repeated before the loud, forceful ending.

Beethoven based the Adagio on the slow movement of a piano quartet he had composed in 1785 but had discarded. Although the movement sounds like a long song, it includes two themes that are stated and then brought back in variation.

The third movement carries the title Menuetto, even though it is not especially dancelike. Rather it maintains a subdued, wistful character throughout, punctuated by a few powerful outbursts of sound.

The Prestissimo shows Beethoven at his violent, furious best. Racing along at a breakneck pace, the movement has a few moments of relaxation that last just long enough to allow performer and listener time to prepare for the next onslaught.

A quick, imperious, though restrained, gesture abruptly opens the **Piano Sonata No. 2 in A, Op. 2, No. 2.** After a lyrical extension, the opening figure returns, this time loud and commanding and continuing with startling dynamic contrasts, until the music slows and the flowing, expressive contrasting theme enters. The working-out of the themes is stormy and agitated, replete with vertiginous changes of dynamics before a comparatively literal review of the two themes.

A deliberate, implacable bass line supports and energizes the noble dignity of the slow-moving Largo appassionato melody. Varied brief interludes make their appearance between returns of the main subject.

While the opening motif of the first movement bears a hint of foreboding, the fleeting figure that starts the Scherzo projects a spirit of gay insouciance, even as Beethoven whips up the music to a crashing climax. The middle section presents a cantabile contrast before the reprise of the first part.

The final movement, organized as a rondo, contains four statements of the theme separated by contrasting interludes. The theme itself is characterized by a meteoric rising arpeggio (shades of the Mannheim rocket), followed by a dizzying downward leap. The minor-mode second interlude strikes particularly hard with its raging anger. The next return of the principal subject replaces the initial arpeggio with a rushing upward scale and adds florid decorations to the melody itself. More excitement ensues before the music subsides to a quiet ending.

Although there were few public concerts in Vienna in the mid-1790s, Beethoven frequently performed as pianist at the homes of aristocrats living in that city. The depth of his expressivity, coupled with his splendid technique, reputedly won him a position as perhaps the most outstanding performer of the time —an assessment with which he probably agreed. Particularly admired as an improviser, he was always winning the contests in which pianists were asked to extemporize on a theme supplied by a noble patron.

Nowhere does this spirit of improvisation, along with the exuberant good spirits of a highly successful young man, come across as clearly as in Beethoven's **Piano Sonata No. 3 in C, Op. 2, No. 3.** Although brilliant and virtuosic in sound, the writing for the piano is so idiomatic and grateful that it is a popular favorite of both audiences and players alike.

In addition to the sheer joy of its musical expressivity, the C major sonata shows Beethoven in complete control of form and structure. The simple opening motif evolves naturally and organically, including some stunning orchestra-like outbursts of sound, until the first theme gives way to the two beguilingly tender and fragile phrases that make up the second subject. A masterly development section propels the music forward to the return of the thematic material. The movement ends with an extended coda that contains a written-out cadenza. (Cadenzas, which are rare in sonatas, were usually left to the performer's improvisatory skill.)

The Adagio brings to mind Beethoven as improviser. One can easily imagine him spontaneously creating the theme at the keyboard and then allowing some subconscious urge to fashion the following contrasting interludes and returns of the theme. Two particularly striking moments stand out: the bold, forceful new start of the theme after its second appearance and the huge dramatic downward jump just before the movement ends.

Beethoven begins the Scherzo in a fugal, imitative texture, which he alternates with passages enlivened by offbeat accents. Some have described the middle section, the Trio, as lacking melody, citing only the rising and falling arpeggios in the right hand and ignoring the melodic line in the left hand.

Fast, vital, and crackling with excitement, the finale stands out as the show movement of the sonata. Exploiting a wide variety of piano techniques, Beethoven dazzles the listener at the same time as he provides a movement of considerable musical pleasure for the player.

The **Piano Sonata No. 4 in E flat. Op. 7,** composed in 1796 and 1797, carries a dedication to Countess Babette von

Keglevics, a young woman who was Beethoven's piano student at the time. Contemporary accounts reveal that Beethoven was in love with her, and that the sonata was then known by its subtitle, "Der Verliebte" ("The Beloved"), although the music itself does not hint at any programmatic content.

The first movement, for example, has scant moments of warmth or lyricism. It is, instead, impassioned in its relentless forward drive and its great sweep and vigor. And, as is so frequently the case in these early sonatas, the movement encompasses some startling dynamic contrasts and a few breathtaking leaps.

In the Largo, Beethoven shows what exquisite, eloquent use he can make of silence. The opening of the theme consists of groups of two or three notes separated by equally long pauses that serve to intensify and heighten the effect of the notes. This section gives way in time to a songful, soulful melody heard over an ongoing staccato accompaniment in the bass. From these two subjects Beethoven spins out the entire intriguing movement.

Too fast for the deliberate tempo of a minuet and lacking the fleeting verve of a scherzo, the third movement seems to be a cross between the two. The wistful first part remains completely involved with the melodic phrase heard at the outset. An agitated and somewhat menacing middle section follows, its melody emerging from the rapid, ongoing figuration. The movement concludes with a shortened reprise of the opening section.

A tender, graceful melody serves as the principal subject of the last movement, a rondo. The first interlude consists of a dialogue between the loud, angry bass and the quiet, placating treble, which continues until they finally agree on a particular turn of melody. After a repeat of the main theme, the second interlude erupts in a fury of rushing notes and rhythmic energy. Beethoven then brings back the first two sections and appends an extended coda before the music quietly fades away.

"Things go well for me; I may even say better and better." So wrote Beethoven in May 1797 to his friend Dr. Franz Wegler, as he won growing success as a composer, pianist, and teacher for the leading families of Vienna. It was around this time, while

Beethoven was enjoying the full flush of professional acceptance and recognition, that he wrote the three sonatas of Op. 10.

All his life, the key of C minor held special significance for Beethoven. Some of his most serious, intense, and dramatic works are in this key, as witness the early Piano Trio, Op. 1, No. 3, and String Trio, Op. 9, No. 3, as well as the "Pathétique" Sonata, String Quartet, Op. 18, No. 4, and Fifth Symphony that came later.

The **Piano Sonata No. 5 in C minor, Op. 10, No. 1,** a passionate and fervid composition, is very much in keeping with Beethoven's C-minor mystique. Beethoven's formal organization in this sonata is of special interest in that all three movements follow sonata-allegro form. But as though to avoid any danger of slackening interest the composer omits the coda in movement one, the development section in movement two, and goes through all the sections of this form (exposition, development, recapitulation, coda) only in movement three.

The rapidly rising first theme of the opening movement immediately establishes its headstrong, impetuous character. Although the second theme emerges as much more songlike, it includes ascending scales that give it the same upward-reaching shape.

After the extroverted first movement, the Adagio molto presents itself as introspective and self-absorbed. Extremely slow in tempo, the movement's character can perhaps best be described as restrained and quiet overall, vanishing finally into inaudibility.

The Finale falls between the first two movements in dynamic range. Bustling and energetic, the movement progresses at a good clip, allowing little time for repose or reflection. Only in the coda does Beethoven allow the tempo to relax for a nostalgic restatement of the second theme. This is followed by a forceful, ingenious combining of the two themes before the quiet conclusion.

One reads that the **Piano Sonata No. 6 in F, Op. 10, No. 2,** was one of Beethoven's favorites—and it is easy to understand why. Just as C minor was his key for serious and profound music, so he chose F major to express the relaxed, jovial side of his personality, often enlivened with many wonderful touches of humor that add to its appeal.

The brief, light, and pithy principal theme of the opening Allegro, with its flip motifs, contributes to an overall comic effect. The second theme follows immediately, but before we have time to absorb the new cantabile melody Beethoven humorously breaks the flow by changing the regular rhythmic pattern and accenting the offbeats. The third or concluding theme continues the playful mood with two delicate, high-pitched three-note fragments answered by low-pitched growls. The exposition ends with three powerful cadential chords. In the development section, instead of working out any of the major themes, Beethoven indulges in a delightful free fantasy on those three notes. To perpetuate the wit of the movement, Beethoven then returns the first theme—but in the wrong key (D instead of F). He soon sets matters right, however, and ends the movement with no further surprises.

After the jolly first movement, Beethoven becomes a bit more serious in the Allegretto. Although structured as a scherzo in three-part form, its more solemn mien, nostalgic character, and deliberate pace allow it to function as a slow movement as well. Mostly quiet and calm, the Allegretto puts into even greater relief the gaiety of the preceding movement and the cheerful movement that is to come next.

Beethoven starts the Presto with a rollicking good tune that he immediately subjects to fugal imitation. Although there is a second theme, distinguished by key rather than any change of melodic character, Beethoven maintains the ongoing polyphonic texture throughout. By treating the all-important main theme in any number of frolicsome, comic ways, Beethoven supplies us with a musical analogue to the verbal puns that he so enjoyed making.

Careful listening to Beethoven's **Piano Sonata No. 7 in D, Op. 10, No. 3**, reveals a number of relationships between the themes within one movement and among the movements. Are these deliberate derivations on Beethoven's part or are they subconscious borrowings? Are they perhaps pure coincidence, brought about by the fact that some of the themes use extremely common turns of melody, such as fragments of scales? In the absence of any comments on the subject by Beethoven and the knowledge that such cross-relationships were not an accepted compositional practice of the time, we are led to assume that the melodic interchanges are either subconscious or coincidental. But, no matter what their origin, one cannot but be acutely aware of the many thematic interconnections in the sonata.

Both principal themes of the first movement, for example, start with four descending notes, a figure that goes on to dominate the movement as it appears in various contexts throughout. The only noticeable exception occurs in the coda, where several times the four notes rise instead of fall and sometimes include a leap instead of progressing only by step.

Beethoven's tempo marking for the second movement indicates both the speed—Largo, literally "broad," but commonly accepted to mean a very slow speed, and the character—*mesto*, meaning "sad" or "mournful." According to Beethoven's friend and student Anton Schindler, the composer said that this movement depicted "the spiritual state of a melancholy man, with all the various nuances of light and shade that make up the picture of melancholy." Indeed, despite the beauty and sensitivity of the writing, this music evokes deep despair, and the intensity of its expression makes the Largo the emotional fulcrum of the entire sonata. Moreover, the second movement is tied to the preceding movement by the descending four-note figure that starts both the second phrase of the principal themes and the opening of the subsidiary theme.

With the ensuing Menuetto, Beethoven allows the bright sunlight to dispel the darkness of the Largo e mesto. Gliding along easily and gracefully, it supplies the perfect antidote to the sorrow that has preceded. Still present, though, is the downward-moving motif in notes 2 through 5 of the main theme.

While the initial four notes of the sonata play a role in the first three movements, the finale grows around the next three notes of that same opening theme. Structured as a tight, concise rondo, the three-note motif pervades the principal subject. Two contrasting interludes are inserted between appearances of the main melody. The brief first interlude, little more than a rapidly rising and descending chromatic scale, and the equally short second interlude, a forceful, agitated section that dies away to the final return of the chief melody, are developed and expanded by Beethoven in the coda before the sonata's quiet close.

Dramatic, impassioned, and intense, the **Piano Sonata No. 8 in C minor, Op. 13, "Pathétique,"** is among the most beloved of all piano sonatas—today as well as in Beethoven's time. It is a member of the group of several outstanding works he wrote in the key of C minor. Beethoven himself called it *"Grande Sonate pathétique,"* and it does indeed capture all the pain and pathos that the subtitle implies. Written when the composer was not yet thirty years old, it moves from the *Sturm und Drang* of the introduction and the febrile body of the first movement, through the consolation of the Adagio cantabile, to the search for succor in the concluding Rondo.

A grim rising motif that is repeatedly cut off, either by a weak drifting-off into silence or by raging, demonic interruptions informs the entire slow introduction to the first movement. Like a coiled spring, the main part of the movement arrives with a rush of high-speed, concentrated energy. At the end of the exposition and again before the coda, Beethoven brings back brief reminders of the introduction, an indication of the importance and integrity of the introduction in relation to the total musical statement.

After the vehement outbreak of the opening movement, the Adagio cantabile offers a serene respite of sublime beauty. A simple, luminous melody gently floats over a murmured accompaniment. The melody appears three times with little change, the repetitions separated by two contrasted episodes—the first with the repeated left-hand notes adding a sense of urgency, the second with a faster accompanying figuration that creates more of a feeling of agitation.

In interpreting the finale, many pianists are strongly tempted to set off at a fast, bright tempo (it is marked Allegro, "fast"), and to play in a light, jaunty style (as the writing seems to indicate). But if the player is mindful—and respectful—of the sonata's subtitle, then he or she chooses a slightly slower tempo and restrains the impulse to make it overly cheerful. Be that as it may, there is no question that the sonata has moved a very considerable distance from the gloom of the opening to the optimism—muted or overt—of the last movement. As is so often the case in his works in C minor, which are almost without exception passionate and somewhat troubled, Beethoven concludes on a positive note of affirmative resolution.

Beethoven composed the two sonatas of Op. 14 in 1798 and 1799, though he may have prepared preliminary sketches four years earlier. According to Anton Schindler, Beethoven commented, "Everyone saw that the two sonatas Op. 14 represented a struggle between two opposing principles, an argument between two persons."

The composer left no clue as to the exact meaning of the "struggle" beyond this enigmatic statement, although it is usually taken to mean the conflict between male and female qualities. The music of the **Piano Sonata No. 9 in E, Op. 14, No. 1,** manifests the opposition in various ways. In the first movement the conflict could be between the freedom of the widely spaced principal theme and the constricted, chromatic subsidiary subject. In the second movement, perhaps it is the clash heard in the juxtaposition of the dark, inward-looking opening and the light, extroverted contrasting section. And in the finale, the tension might reside in the difference of character and style of the main theme and the interspersed episodes.

Despite the mystery of Beethoven's remark, almost everyone agrees that the gentle and modest E major charms with wit, grace, and intimacy, while offering quite a contrast to the intense "Pathétique."

A few points of especial interest stand out: over a sketch for the development section of the first movement, Beethoven wrote, *"ohne das Thema durchzuführen"* ("Without working through the theme"). While the development starts like a traditional exploration of the principal subject, the composer soon introduces a completely new melody, which he then expands. This is followed, without any further development, by a brief transition based on the first theme and the forceful start of the recapitulation, which reviews the movement's two themes.

Since the sonata is too short and small in scale for an extended, profound slow movement, Beethoven, in effect, combines the slow and dance movements. By imposing a leisurely pace on a minuet, he produces a particularly appealing hybrid movement.

The compact Rondo is predominantly quiet and subdued. Only in the second contrasting episode—an agitated section of rapid figuration, with the melody emerging as accents within the rushing flood of notes—does Beethoven let loose with some big, loud virtuosic piano playing, for the first time in the entire sonata.

If it is difficult to spot the two opposing principles in Op. 14, No. 1, it is even harder to locate them in the companion work, the **Piano Sonata No. 10 in G, Op. 14, No. 2.** (Some pianists program the two sonatas as a recital group.) Although Beethoven's exact meaning may elude us, we can still enjoy the sonata as a warm, inviting miniature with delightful humorous overtones that has the remarkable quality of being able to captivate and completely command our attention without ever raising its voice.

Rhythmically ambiguous, fluid, and flowing, the extremely attractive main theme easily dominates the entire first movement with the subsidiary theme maintaining the same Apollonian calm as the opening. Rising to some restrained climaxes in the development, Beethoven then brings back the opening—but in the wrong key. After continuing in this direction for a while, Beethoven returns the first theme in its proper key and ends the movement quietly.

As in Op. 14, No. 1, the scope of the sonata does not allow for a major slow movement. In its place Beethoven writes a simple, crisp, marchlike tune, which he subjects to three variations. In Variation 1 the melody remains largely confined to the left hand, while the right hand adds a descant above it. Variation 2 atomizes the theme into a pattern of short offbeat chords. And the final section weaves a smooth variant of the melody into a rapidly moving figuration. Beethoven's sense of humor emerges at the movement's conclusion, when he follows a series of very soft chords with the loud explosion of the final chord.

Why did Beethoven entitle the last movement Scherzo, when it is so obviously a rondo? Eric Blom convincingly argues that

Beethoven started to write a four-movement work with this as a true scherzo, but not being able to adapt the thematic material to that form cast it as a concluding rondo. Jocular and playful in spirit, the movement seems to take the literal meaning of *scherzo,* "joke" in Italian. Its jesting theme does not reveal its meter easily. And the rude outbursts of sound, the unexpected moments of silence, and the music's disappearance at the end with an insouciant flip of the wrist, all contribute to the jovial character.

The year 1800 marked an important transition for Beethoven. Around then, Beethoven became aware that he was losing his hearing and began to suffer all the fear, anguish, and mental upset that this discovery occasioned. At about this time, too, he began to break free of the influence of his two great predecessors, Haydn and Mozart. Mechanical improvements in the piano also led him to conceive his keyboard music more for the new instrument and less for the harpsichord and its immediate descendants. And, of course, 1800 also marked the birth of a new century, bringing with it a sense of renewal and rebirth.

Beethoven completed his **Piano Sonata No. 11 in B flat, Op. 22,** at this important time. The music exhibits an intensification of expression, and a mingling of nostalgia for the past and anticipation of what lay ahead, including greater piano-specific writing with fuller exploitation of the instrument's potentialities. Beethoven was particularly proud of this sonata; when he submitted it to Hoffmeister, his publisher, in January 1801, he wrote, "This sonata, most beloved and worthy brother, is something special." Despite Beethoven's high opinion, however, the work has never been very widely performed.

One explanation for its lack of favor may be the themes of the first movement, which lack distinction and any truly memorable features. The first subject starts with a call to attention, albeit at a soft dynamic level, and then goes on to various other motifs, some of which are based on brilliant pianistic figurations. Continuing from the scale line with which the first group of themes ends, the second subject begins as an elaboration of an F chord and goes on from there. The exposition ends with a puissant, stentorian rising and falling line that plays an important role in the following development section. After coming to a full stop, Beethoven provides a regular recapitulation of both themes, but ends the movement rather abruptly without a coda.

The way that Beethoven spins out its substantial length, and the freedom of its chromatic alterations gives the main melody of the Adagio the character of a highly romantic nocturne or impromptu. This movement, more than any other, points ahead to the expressive new directions music would be taking in the dawning nineteenth century.

The sharply contrasting Menuetto, although filled with great grace and charm, seems by comparison rather bland, pallid, and reactionary. But Beethoven has a surprise waiting in store for us. During the middle part, the minor-mode Trio, he whips up an exciting emotional maelstrom, with the left hand rushing forward without stop, while the right hand cuts through the flood of notes with spiky offbeat accents. Then, after the Trio's onslaught, how wonderful is the simple and elegant return of the Menuetto.

One can almost hear Beethoven taking leave of his musical past in the concluding Rondo. Although organized in a standard form, the writing has an uncharacteristic looseness and freedom and avoids the crystalline clarity and propulsive energy that is usually associated with music composed at this time.

Just as Op. 22 represents a transition from Beethoven's early to middle period, the 1801 **Piano Sonata No. 12 in A flat, Op. 26,** marks the first work in the new style. Quite clearly, it shows Beethoven setting off in a new, forward-looking direction.

The structure of the opening movement represents the first departure. Instead of the traditional sonata-allegro form, Beethoven begins with a theme and variations. Although he had some precedent in the first movement of Mozart's A major sonata (K. 331), opening with a theme and variation movement still signaled a bold break with the past. After stating the ingratiating theme, Beethoven subjects it to five variations—none of which strays very far from the original. Variation 1 adds arpeggios on the first beat of each measure; Variation 2 comprises a rapid-fire dialogue between the two hands; Variation 3 continues the two-hand dialogue at a slower pace and in the minor mode, and constitutes the expressive climax of the movement; Variation 4 fragments the cantabile melody by displacing alternate phrases up an octave; and Variation 5 elaborates the original tune. The movement ends with a brief coda in which Beethoven introduces a completely new, attractive melody.

Rather than following with a traditional slow movement, Beethoven places the Scherzo next. Although it starts quietly, the music develops a great deal of nervous, agitated energy. Beethoven purposely keeps the middle part, the Trio, calm and reassuring; its repeated rhythm effectively setting into sharp relief the opening and its shortened repetition at the end.

Beethoven sat with the composer Ferdinando Paër at the June 6, 1801, Vienna premiere (or perhaps a subsequent performance) of Paër's opera *Achilles.* When the ever confident Beethoven heard the funeral music played on the death of Patroclus, he presumably leaned over to Paër and whispered, "How beautiful, how interesting! I shall have to compose that." And so he did—first as the slow movement of Op. 26 and then, three years later, in his "Eroica" Symphony. Although Beethoven called the piano sonata movement *"Marcia funebre sulla morte d'un eroe"* ("Funeral Music on the Death of a Hero"), he never identified the "hero," nor did he provide any clue as to whether or not he had someone specific in mind. Maintaining the dotted-rhythm (long/short) pattern throughout and staying low in the piano's range, Beethoven establishes and sustains the movement's mournful, grieving tone. Before the opening makes a return appearance there is a brief contrasting episode, in which some commentators hear echoes of muffled rolling drums and guns fired in salute.

After the solemnity of the Funeral March, Beethoven ends the sonata with a somewhat more optimistic rondo. But instead of structuring it around an easily recognized, clearly defined melody with sharply contrasting interludes, Beethoven writes the entire movement as a sort of toccata—a "touching"-of-the-keys piece. Beethoven seemingly revels in the sheer pleasure of putting fingers to keyboard and unleashes a rippling flood of notes that finally reaches an abrupt, unexpected ending.

By entitling each of the two sonatas of Op. 27 (composed in 1801) "Sonata quasi una Fantasia" ("Sonata, almost a fantasy"),

Beethoven puts the listener on notice that these works are not going to be like the typical sonatas of the period. And indeed, right from the start, the **Piano Sonata No. 13 in E flat, Op. 27, No. 1,** parts company with all of Beethoven's previous works in the form.

Far from the expected fast and substantial sonata-allegro movement, the first movement of the E-flat sonata starts at a slow tempo with a simple tune that brings to mind a stately dance from an eighteenth-century suite. After ruminating a short while on this subject, Beethoven proceeds without a break into what sounds like a robust German peasant dance, its bare melody embellished with rapid figurations. This soon gives way to a shortened reprise of the opening section, creating a movement that may be short in profundity yet is highly appealing in its innocent beauty.

In another departure from standard practice, Beethoven directs that the second movement, a scherzo, follow without pause. Particularly striking is the fact that no true melody graces either the opening scherzo section, the middle trio, or the return of the scherzo.

The justification for the paucity of melodic content in the scherzo is made obvious in the Adagio, which also continues without pause. The impact of the Adagio theme—one of the most expressive, emotional, and luminous that Beethoven ever penned—is all the more powerful after an essentially themeless movement. In effect, Beethoven does little more than state and repeat the predominant Adagio theme and add a short cadenza before going on to the connected finale.

Once more going against the established pattern, Beethoven makes the last movement the most significant, intricate, and profound part of the sonata. Forging an organizational scheme that falls between a rondo and sonata-allegro, the music surges forward with great fire and intensity until, near the end, it builds to a forceful climax, out of which emerges a recollection of the Adagio theme. A short cadenza leads to the brilliant coda that concludes the work.

Among the most familiar pieces of music that Beethoven ever wrote is the first movement of his **Piano Sonata No. 14 in**

C-sharp minor, Op. 27, No. 2, "Moonlight,"—and the work most surrounded with misinformation. Contrary to most assumptions, Beethoven did not write the music to evoke the mood of a moonlit night. Composed in 1801 and published in 1802, the subtitle was conceived thirty years later by music critic H.F.L. Rellstab, who wrote that the music reminded him of "a boat passing the scenery of Lake Lucerne in the moonlight." Now permanently attached to the music, the subtitle persists despite the fact that Beethoven never even visited Lake Lucerne. Moreover, not by the wildest stretch of the imagination is it possible to associate the second and third movements with such a nocturnal scene.

Nor was the "Moonlight" intended as a love song to the dedicatee of the piece, Countess Giulietta Guicciardi. It is true that Beethoven was infatuated with the Countess and planned to show his love by dedicating a piece, his Rondo, Op. 51, No. 2, to her. But he changed his mind when it became necessary, for political reasons, to inscribe a work to Princess Lichnowsky on very short notice. Ever the pragmatist, Beethoven addressed the Rondo to Lichnowsky and then, to make amends, dedicated the "Moonlight" Sonata to Giulietta.

And finally, despite the sonata's immense popularity, Beethoven had reservations about the work. "Everybody is always talking about the C-sharp minor sonata," he complained to his pupil Carl Czerny in 1802. "Surely I have written better things."

Composed with the same subtitle, "Sonata quasi una Fantasia," as Op. 27, No. 1, the "Moonlight" finds Beethoven rising to the highest peaks of creativity and innovation, unfettered by the traditional restrictions. This achievement is most obvious in the sonata's overall organization. Unlike a typical sonata of the time that is in four movements—a big, important sonata-allegro, a slow movement, a scherzo, and a fast, lightweight finale—the "Moonlight" starts with the slow movement, follows with a scherzo, and ends with a movement that has the length, significance, and intensity of an opening movement.

The familiar Adagio sostenuto conveys the quality of a masterly keyboard improvisation, one that convincingly evokes the feelings and emotions associated with great pain and yearning.

The movement captures all the passion and intensity of expression that appeared decades later in the highly romantic "character pieces" of Schubert, Chopin, Schumann, and Mendelssohn.

Liszt calls the second movement, which follows without pause, a "flower between two abysses." It is, in fact, a comforting interlude of relaxation between the agony of the Adagio sostenuto and the fierce energy of the upcoming Presto agitato.

A feverish whirl of notes that quickly races to climax and then starts all over again, the Presto agitato comes hard on the heels of the preceding movement, surging ever forward with an almost manic energy. (Although not so marked in the score, performers usually do not break between the movements.) Written much like a typical first movement, the Presto constitutes the longest and most important part of the sonata. Structured in sonata-allegro form, the first subject is less a melody than a series of frenzied arpeggios, and the second subject, although somewhat calmer, still continues the rapid figuration that gives this finale its powerful, driving impetus. Beethoven caps off the movement with an extended coda that includes some cadenzalike passages before building up to the stunning final chords.

The subtitle of Beethoven's **Piano Sonata No. 15 in D, Op. 28, "Pastoral"** (1801), was chosen by music publisher August Cranz. Although not of Beethoven's invention, the term aptly describes the peaceful, bucolic quality of the music, particularly the fourth movement. The appellation is appropriate, too, because the repeated bass note that accompanies the principal themes of both outside movements was associated at that time with music of a rustic character. The "Pastoral" is, incidentally, the last of Beethoven piano sonatas to follow the traditional four-movement scheme; all the subsequent sonatas contain either two or three movements.

Over the perseverating bass note Beethoven introduces the tranquil first subject, which he follows with the equally subdued second theme, recognized by its somewhat waltzlike rhythm. After repeating the two themes, Beethoven devotes the entire development section to the first theme in an ingenious way—presenting and repeating the entire theme, its last four measures, its last two measures, and finally only its last measure, on which he fixates for some time before coming to a quiet close. A brief transition section then leads to the return of the two themes and a concluding coda.

According to Carl Czerny, the Andante, with its simple, wistful melody and unflagging bass line, was a particular favorite of the composer and he performed it often. The contrasting middle section abruptly introduces a new character, but the movement concludes with an ornamented restatement of the first section, which creates the illusion of being the same as the opening, yet different.

The Scherzo, a playful miniature, contains a jocular main theme basically consisting of three descending octave leaps. The central Trio includes two short melodic phrases that Beethoven presents twice in one particular order and then two more times in the reverse order. A shortened return of the opening then neatly rounds off this delightful little romp.

The finale, perhaps the most peacefully pastoral section, moves gently along, shaped by a few puissant climaxes. Combining elements of a rondo and of sonata-allegro form, the movement builds at the end to a brilliant, high-speed conclusion.

In 1802, when Beethoven was writing the three sonatas of Op. 31, he remarked to his friend, violinist Wenzel Krumpholtz, "I am not satisfied with my previous works; from here on I shall follow a new path." One can only conjecture that the new elements in the **Piano Sonata No. 16 in G, Op. 31, No. 1,** the first of the three, are the greater simplicity and lightness of touch, a growing involvement with certain technical details, and some obvious touches of humor and geniality; there is also apparently little attempt at profundity or seriousness.

The lively Allegro vivace immediately catches one's attention with a strange effect. Could it be a coordination problem between the pianist's two hands? Over and over again the right hand seems to arrive at the downbeat a fraction of a second ahead of the left hand, in what Eric Blom calls a musical "stutter." Beethoven maintains the initial good spirits with the second subject, a sprightly little rhythmic tune that passes from hand to hand. The remainder of the movement proceeds quite regularly—an animated working out of the two themes, their restatement, and a coda to wrap it all up.

Most Beethoven slow movements tend to strive for intense expressivity, but the slow movement here seems more concerned with poise and elegance than with emotional depth. One striking feature of this movement is the use of long trills (rapid alternation between two adjacent notes) as a way of creating the illusion of sustained long notes on the piano, an instrument in which each individual note starts to fade as soon as it is sounded. Essentially monothematic, the melody with the trills dominates this movement.

Rather than dazzle with speed and brilliance, the Rondo makes its point by presenting a warm and smiling countenance. Beethoven contributes to the overall good humor by allowing the principal theme to run out of steam near the end. After several unsuccessful attempts to get cranked up again, a long trill starts in the bass and the music speeds off to a whirlwind close.

The **Piano Sonata No. 17 in D minor, Op. 31, No. 2,** the most personal and deeply felt of Op. 31, resounds with the anguish and black despair that the thirty-two-year-old composer was enduring and which he expressed so eloquently in his famous Heiligenstadt Testament. The Testament, a soul-searing letter to his brothers, written in October 1802 but never sent, describes the unendurable pain Beethoven was suffering because of his ever worsening deafness. The words even suggest that he was contemplating suicide as a way of ending his misery.

The subtitle "Tempest," which is occasionally attached to this sonata, springs from Beethoven's reply to his pupil and friend Anton Schindler, who once asked the composer about the sonata's meaning and was told, "Just read Shakespeare's *Tempest.*" The fact that the piece is indeed stormy, while Shakespeare's play (despite its title) is not, has led to much speculation about Beethoven's real intention. Does "Tempest" refer only to the play's title? Does it suggest irony? Or does it imply relationships between themes in the sonata and characters in Shakespeare's play? Unfortunately, Beethoven left no clues to his meaning beyond the music itself.

The four solemn notes that open the sonata sound like the

start of a slow introduction. But suddenly a fast, busy flurry of notes intrudes. Beethoven next transposes the four deliberate notes and the ensuing bustle up two notes higher, and then proceeds to a bass-soprano conversation, with the bass statements consisting of nothing more than the inital four notes played much faster. The subsidiary theme that follows has two parts—a lightly tripping melody and a stubborn progression of block chords that interrupts the flow. This presentation of the themes, including the slow opening, comes again, to be followed by the development section, which concerns itself almost exclusively with the low-high dialogue. Beethoven ends the development with a free recitative based on the all-important opening notes and, after a short transition, returns only the second group of themes before quietly ending the movement.

The emotional high point of the sonata, the Adagio, can be simply described: a warm, poignant melody, though with a slightly troubled cast, is followed by a tune of great poise and confidence. Both melodies are then repeated with some slight elaboration.

The agitation and turmoil that characterize the third movement project a feeling of unease and disquiet, rather than of strength and energy. Underscoring this impression is the sudden, almost pathetic falling away of the music at the very end.

While the D minor sonata can be construed as an outgrowth of the torment Beethoven felt as he came to accept his irreversible deafness, the **Piano Sonata No. 18 in E flat, Op. 31, No. 3,** on the other hand, sounds as though it was penned by a carefree, self-assured soul. In it Beethoven seems perfectly content to adapt the musical vocabulary of the past to his own creative purposes, rather than to seek out new modes of expression. The result is a bright, clear work, with virtually no hint of the angst that informs so many of Beethoven's other compositions.

Despite some strange, intriguing harmonic touches at the outset, the first movement seems pervaded by joy and cheerfulness set forth with great certainty of purpose and clarity of structure. For example, the end of the principal subject is unequivocally marked by four forceful descending octave jumps. Also, the cheerful little eighteenth-century tune that follows, with its "hiccup" interruption, is plainly different from what has come before. The development of the two themes and their return are masterfully handled with simplicity and lucidity.

Even though it is entitled Scherzo, the second movement bears little resemblance to typical works in that form. It has two rather than three beats to a measure; it is in sonata-allegro rather than scherzo (ABA) form, and it is somewhat slower in tempo than usual. Perhaps best described as a tantalizing, albeit eccentric, movement, its success depends to a very large extent on the performer's strict observance of the rather quirky dynamic and tempo indications.

Where one would expect a slow movement, Beethoven places a Menuetto. Mindful of tradition, though, he makes it slow and graceful, with a wonderfully vocal melody in the opening and closing sections, and a more pianistic theme in the central Trio.

Filled with good humor and unforced gaiety, the last movement provides a vigorous conclusion to this most winsome of pieces.

Were it not for the initiative of Beethoven's brother Caspar, the world would likely not know of the **Piano Sonata No. 19 in G minor, Op. 49, No. 1**, and **Piano Sonata No. 20 in G, Op. 49, No. 2**. Beethoven composed these two works around the year 1796, but never submitted them for publication. Caspar, though, took it on himself to send the two manuscripts to the Viennese publisher Bureau des Arts et de l'Industrie, who put them out in 1805—to the composer's annoyance, since he felt that he had moved far beyond them in style and maturity in the intervening nine years.

Both works can be considered miniatures, more sonatinas than full-blown sonatas. Containing but two movements each, they make few technical demands on the performer and are consequently favorites of students and amateurs, as well as the many professionals who appreciate the plenitude of delights these modest compositions have to offer.

The attraction of the G minor's rather slow first movement resides in its warmth and convivality; there is no bombast, no baring of the soul, no alternation of tension and relaxation—just pleasant, inviting music making.

The second and last movement, a rondo, has a livelier and more spirited nature, and appears in the major rather than minor mode. Written with much more rhythmic drive than the preceding movement, the rondo manages to rise to a few climactic high points.

Curiously enough, Op. 49, No. 2, was originally published without dynamic indications; all markings in modern editions were supplied either by editors or by famous performers in the past. Of the two movements, the first may be considered a vigorous exercise that presents a particularly explicit display of sonata-allegro form stripped to its essentials.

Beethoven was especially partial to the melody of the Menuetto; he later (despite the lower opus number) used it in his Septet, Op. 20 (1799–1800). Structured as a rondo, rather than as a minuet, the Menuetto cannot help but charm the listener and performer.

Within a few years of 1800, Beethoven wrote five major works that he dedicated to outstanding contemporary figures and that are usually identified by the individual's name: the "Kreutzer" piano and violin sonata, Op. 47 (1803), for Rodolphe Kreutzer, the famous French violinist; the three "Rasoumowsky" string quartets, Op. 59 (1806), for Count Andreas Rasoumowsky, Russian ambassador to the Imperial Court at Vienna; and the **Piano Sonata No. 21 in C, Op. 53, "Waldstein"** (1804), for Count Ferdinand von Waldstein, longtime friend and patron of Beethoven's.

Although the first movement of the "Waldstein" starts very quietly (as do each of the subsequent movements), the persistent, reiterated chords immediately suggest that we are undertaking a musical odyssey of great significance. Indeed, as Beethoven sets forth the two principal themes—the first capping each phrase of agitated, repeated chords with a bass-line comment and treble retort, and the block chords of the second introducing a wondrous feeling of calm and repose into the nervous proceedings—a sense of spaciousness, scope, and generosity of gesture emerges, which was not evident in the earlier sonatas. After the expansive statement and repetition of the thematic material, Beethoven allows time for a full-scale working through of the melodies, a regular return of both subjects, and a lengthy coda for the conclusion.

The fact that Beethoven discarded the slow movement he originally wrote for this sonata has led to some speculation that he did so at the suggestion of Ferdinand Ries, his student and friend. Others hold that Beethoven himself decided that the section was too long and mild for the overall architecture of the sonata. In any case, he removed his first effort at a slow movement and published it separately under the title "Andante favori"; in its stead he wrote a very short movement that he entitled Introduzione. The movement really is an introduction since its many mysterious silences and ambiguities build up a tension that is finally relieved by the warmth and affability of the Rondo finale, which follows without pause.

Beethoven did not write the principal melody of the Rondo easily; the many sketches he left show the mighty struggle he had to wage before achieving the superb final result, which at times captivates with its pellucid beauty and at other times inspires with its exuberance. As contrasts to this theme, Beethoven inserts two different stormy, aggressive episodes in the minor mode. At the very end he justifies the moderate, rather than fast, tempo by practically doubling the speed for a dazzling, virtuosic conclusion.

The **Piano Sonata No. 22 in F, Op. 54**, almost suggests that the composer, exhausted by the effort to produce the large-scale "Waldstein" sonata, wanted to relax with his next work in the form. The F major does indeed represent a respite between the "Waldstein" and the "Appassionata"—two towering undertakings. Considerably shorter in length and more modest than either of these works, the F major nevertheless has its own charm and, at times, gentle humor. Still, the Op. 54 has never really caught the fancy of performers or audiences and consequently is rarely played or heard.

Marked to be played in the tempo of a minuet, the first movement has some characteristics of that dance, but with elements of variation superimposed. Essentially the movement alternates a rather relaxed, wistful theme and its variants with a bold, highly accented section, which is also heard in variation.

Although scientists long ago gave up the hope of ever building a perpetual motion machine, composers never tire of re-creating the phenomenon in musical terms. Written with rushing sixteenth notes throughout and essentially with just single notes in both hands, the second and final movement of Op. 54 winningly exemplifies this genre—speeding forward from its quiet opening to the still faster climactic ending.

The **Piano Sonata No. 23 in F minor, Op. 57, "Appassionata,"** completed in 1806, has become universally known by its subtitle, which was the invention of publisher August Cranz and with no evidence of the composer's approval. "Appassionata," however, is an appropriate sobriquet, since the music throbs with intense emotional excitement, particularly in the two outer movements.

The sonata opens softly in a low range; one senses, though, that Beethoven is restraining a melody that, given free rein, would be far more vociferous. The phrase occurs twice, moving up one note for the repetition, both coming before several soundings of the famous four-note rhythmic motto of Beethoven's Fifth Symphony—short, short, short, long—the one that Beethoven is reported to have described as fate knocking at the door. While this may indeed be a programmatic reference to the inexorable working of destiny, the composer may also have used it for strictly musical reasons. An explosive outburst ushers in a free expansion of the theme, alternating whispered phrases and thunderous replies. After a brief bridge passage the second theme appears, similar in rhythm to the first, but calmer and more self-possessed at the beginning, becoming more frenzied in time. Beethoven develops and returns both themes with great ardor and excitement, but reserves the overwhelming climax for the extended coda that ends the movement.

The Andante con moto presents a completely different character than the first movement. Its simple and not particularly distinctive theme is followed by four variations in which the theme is, first, rhythmically fragmented into a syncopated pattern; second, divided into sixteenth notes; third, intensified in mood, and further divided into thirty-second notes; and fourth, returned to its original state for closure.

Two held chords provide a connection to the finale, a highly spirited movement that drives forward with irresistible vitality, now soft, now loud, but never losing its propulsive energy. Although it is in sonata-allegro form, the second theme does not depart much from the character of the preceding melody; as in the first movement, the climax comes in the high-speed, forceful coda.

After creating such grandiose, *concertante* works as the "Waldstein" and "Appassionata," Beethoven, in effect, relaxed for a few years, until 1809, when he produced Opp. 78, 79, and 81a, three of his outstanding middle-period sonatas. The first of the three, the **Piano Sonata No. 24 in F sharp, Op. 78,** finds Beethoven still in a mellow, reposeful mood, with little exuberance or defiance, and few expressions of despair. Of short length and limited emotional range, Op. 78 is an amiable piece whose obvious charms have made it a popular repertoire selection. Although dedicated to Therese von Brunswick, one of the important loves of Beethoven's life, there is little in the music to convey the deep attraction she held for him.

The sonata opens as though it is starting with a slow movement. But the tempo soon picks up speed, introducing the placid principal theme of a regular first movement. After building to a climax, Beethoven pauses briefly and then presents the flowing subsidiary subject. The short working-out section revolves solely around the first theme, before being followed by the recapitulation, in which the opening theme is further expanded. The movement ends with a short coda.

The second and final movement, a playful caprice with irrepressible good spirits, is focused on two distinct themes: the first starting with a loud-soft dialogue that goes on to rapid passagework and the second with repeated meteoric ascents followed by soft murmurings. Having put these two ideas through their paces, Beethoven stops all forward motion with two held chords before plunging ahead to the abrupt ending.

The **Piano Sonata No. 25 in G, Op. 79,** the second of the three sonatas Beethoven composed in 1809, and perhaps the most modest of the group, was dubbed by the composer *Sonate facile ou sonatine* ("Easy Sonata or Sonatina"). The work's detached and impersonal air gives the impression of an un-characteristic lack of personal involvement on Beethoven's part.

By entitling the first movement Presto alla tedesca ("Fast, in the German manner"), Beethoven refers to the style of the *Ländler,* the old German and Austrian country dance that was precursor to the waltz. Even though it is written in triple meter, the movement is played with but one accented beat per measure and maintains a dancelike rhythmic swing.

The short, simple, and technically undemanding middle movement brings to mind a gently lilting barcarolle—the boat song associated with Venetian gondoliers.

Bright and perky, the high-spirited Vivace provides a fitting conclusion to this delightful little sonata.

Beethoven affixed his own subtitles to two piano sonatas: He named the Op. 13 the "Pathétique," a reference to the general character of the work, and he called the **Piano Sonata No. 26 in E flat, Op. 81a** "Das Lebewohl, die Abwesenheit, das Wieder-sehn" ("Farewell, Absence, Reunion"). Such music, which seeks to convey an impression of a definite image, scene, or event, is known as program music. The sonata represents the only programmatic piano sonata that Beethoven wrote.

As a matter of fact, the program of Op. 81a is so important to the music that Beethoven inscribed the syllables *Le-be-wohl* over the first three notes of the piece. Ironically enough, although the composer supplied a German subtitle for the work and wrote the first word in German on the music, the publisher saw fit (to Beethoven's very considerable annoyance) to translate the subtitle into French—"Les Adieux, l'Absence et le Retour." And to compound the indignity, the sonata is now usually referred to as "Les Adieux."

(The strange opus number, 81a, comes from the fact that Beethoven was writing for two publishers at the time. To keep his music in chronological order he was forced to call the sonata Op. 81a and his Sextet for Strings and Horns, Op. 81b.)

The inspiration for the sonata—and the basis of the program—was the flight from Vienna of Beethoven's dear friend, patron, and sometime pupil Archduke Rudolph, who departed Austria when the French invaded on May 4, 1809, and stayed away until peace was declared on October 14 of the same year.

Beethoven began composing the sonata soon after the archduke's hasty withdrawal. The slow introduction to the first movement, "Farewell," starts with the descending three-note motto *Le-be-wohl*. (The similarity to "Three Blind Mice" is purely coincidental!) The way in which the notes are harmonized creates a posthorn call—an obvious reference to the archduke's carriage trip away from Vienna. In the main part of the movement, the head of the first theme fragments the motto in a fast, busy presentation. Played lightly and high on the keyboard, the second theme also emerges clearly as a varied restatement of the three downward-moving notes of the motto. After treating the two themes in a regular manner, Beethoven ends the movement with a lengthy coda in which the *Le-be-wohl* motto becomes a dialogue between the two hands, possibly a musical expression of Beethoven and the archduke making their farewells.

The gentle and reflective slow movement, "Absence," composed during the summer of 1809 while the archduke was away, strongly suggests the composer's musings on the absence of his friend. In keeping with the program, the music takes the form of a single, isolated melody line with accompaniment, a soulful-sounding demonstration of Beethoven's loneliness.

Without pause the finale, "Reunion," suddenly and surprisingly explodes into opulent and sonorous sound. After a few resonant phrases, the quiet principal subject appears, first in the right hand and then in the left, which may represent the coming together of the composer and the aristocrat. Some exultant musical fireworks and a passage that reminds one of gaily tolling church bells precedes the emergence of the subdued subsidiary theme, with both hands playing musically interesting material— perhaps another demonstration of the happy reunion of the two men. The movement proceeds with high spirits and ebullient cheerfulness until the coda, when the tempo slows for a brief and sober reflection on the archduke's return. This momentary sobriety soon gives way to a most impressive conclusion.

Like the E-flat sonata, the **Piano Sonata No. 27 in E minor, Op. 90,** bears some connection outside the music, but the link is much more tenuous. Beethoven dedicated the sonata, which he completed in August 1814, to Count Moritz von Lichnowsky, a friend and patron who had divorced his first wife and was about to marry again. When the count asked Beethoven the meaning of the sonata, the composer reportedly gave a "boisterous laugh" and replied that the first movement depicted the "struggle between head and heart" and the second a "conversation with the loved one."

Did Beethoven's laughter mean that he did not take Lichnowsky's question seriously and gave a flip, sarcastic answer? Or was he, in fact, truly describing his musical intention? Actually, the E minor piano sonata is a wonderful piece, any way you approach it. As almost everyone agrees, the first movement does indeed project a feeling of struggle and quest, while the following movement bespeaks resolution and acceptance.

For those who take Beethoven's comment to Lichnowsky literally, the sonata opening can be conceived as the alternation of a strong, forthright "head" phrase and a sweet, tender "heart" phrase, after which Beethoven concentrates on expanding the second, the "heart" motif. The remainder of the movement, however, concisely traverses the standard sections of first-movement form. The only point out of the ordinary may be the surprise ending, which is not prepared either by slowing down before or by adding a few closing chords afterward; it just stops.

Somewhat slower in tempo than the first, the second movement projects an atmosphere of gentleness and lyricism, despite some forceful moments. Although organized as a rondo, the development of the themes gives the impression of the sonata-allegro form. The main theme occurs a total of four times before reaching the abrupt ending, which is as completely unexpected as was the close of the first movement.

The **Piano Sonata No. 28 in A, Op. 101,** marks Beethoven's entry into his last and—in the view of most—greatest period of composition. In the eight years from 1816 to 1822 Beethoven wrote his incredible final five piano sonatas. This came at a time when the composer was completely deaf and therefore suffering social isolation, was afflicted with serious health problems, and was tormented by the responsibility of caring for his troublesome nephew, Carl. In spite of the anguish and heartache in his personal life, Beethoven's music became infused with a higher level of spirituality, a kind of otherworldliness, that seems to transcend the human-to-human communication of his earlier works. The technical aspects of composition and the physical limitations of the instrument became much less significant; his goal seems to have been pure, unfettered expression.

Composed in November 1816, the Op. 101 sonata does not merit special consideration because it scales any emotional heights or because it plumbs the hidden recesses of the human soul with extraordinary depth and sensitivity. Rather, its notable features are great formal freedom, much greater use of polyphonic texture, and the appearance of considerable dissonance.

Suave and lyrical, the extremely short first movement almost never raises its voice above a whisper as it gently ambles along on its musical journey. Although it is in traditional sonata-allegro form, the various themes and their manipulations flow so effortlessly and seamlessly into one another that the listener tends to agree with Richard Wagner who called it an example of endless melody.

Instead of a scherzo, Beethoven places a march second. Its rough, rude onset is jarring and the shock is intensified by the occasional striking dissonances. The music drives actively and impatiently forward with the dotted (long-short) rhythm predominant. The middle section is marked *dolce* ("sweetly"), even though the writing does not easily allow the performer to achieve that character. The highly polyphonic texture, mostly canonic, has the two hands playing the same musical line, but starting at different times like the well-known round "Frère Jacques." A reprise of the march ends the movement.

Beethoven directs that the short slow movement be played softly throughout. He marks it *"Mit einer Saite"* (literally "With one string"; in practice, with the soft pedal held down). Near the end, Beethoven quotes the first-movement opening and instructs the player to gradually release the soft pedal.

Following without a break, the finale emerges as the longest, most complex, and most fully realized movement of the sonata— the climax of the entire piece. With its angry and defiant nature, this movement is distinguished by much intricate counterpoint. The most striking part, the development, includes a four-voice fugue based on the principal theme of the movement.

The **Piano Sonata No. 19 in B flat, Op. 106, "Hammer-klavier,"** widely acknowledged to be Beethoven's greatest piano sonata, remains one of the towering musical masterworks of all time in spite of its particularly senseless subtitle. Around the time the sonata was composed, Beethoven became convinced that the piano was really a German invention and he wanted to replace the Italian-derived name, pianoforte, with the more fitting German term for the same instrument. He therefore named both his Opp. 101 and 106 sonatas "Grosse Sonate für das Hammerklavier" ("Grand Sonata for the Piano"). Although both sonatas were for the *hammerklavier*—a name that means nothing more than piano—the subtitle stuck only to the Op. 106 sonata.

Beethoven composed the "Hammerklavier" over the period of a year and a half, starting in 1818. Evidence that Beethoven realized its worth right from the start was his comment to Carl Czerny while working on the music: "I am now writing a sonata that will be my greatest."

With its imperious, defiant opening phrase and the lyrical, almost supplicating, response, Beethoven delineates the emotional range of the first movement. Conceived in broad, spacious terms, the movement has two groups of contrasting themes instead of two individual themes, each group containing a variety of musical ideas and gestures. A striking feature of the expansive development section is, near its start, a fugal section based on the opening motif. A free recapitulation and a highly dramatic coda bring this most imposing movement to an end.

One guesses that after this mighty opening Beethoven was reluctant to go on to a serious, emotional, and equally demanding slow movement. Perhaps that is why he placed the three-part Scherzo next. A little rhythmic figure that occurs by count thirty-four times completely dominated the capricious first part. So strong is the propulsive power of Beethoven's writing, though, that the listener loses sight of the repetition and is swept along by the musical current. The middle section features a cantabile melody that is played twice by the right hand with a flowing accompaniment in the left, and both times is then reversed, giving the melody to the left hand and the accompaniment to the right. An impertinent interruption by a fast section in two-beat meter in the midst of the three-beat meter and a run from the bottom to the top of the keyboard act as a bridge to the return of the opening Scherzo section.

The profound, emotional, and extremely moving and affective Adagio sostenuto comes next. Despite its considerable length—twenty minutes or thereabouts—the music cannot but grip listeners and hold them completely in its thrall. Twice Beethoven inserts a ghostly waltzlike section that sets into even greater relief the overwhelming feeling of resignation and acceptance that suffuses the movement.

As at the end of the second movement, Beethoven had again to be very careful in what followed so sublime a musical statement. A gay, happy rondo would just not do. To effect a transition, Beethoven begins the last movement with a slow, free fantasy. Then he fashions the fast movement itself into a titanic three-voice fugue. Placing incredible demands on the listener, and even more on the performer, this fugue proves the equal of the other magnificent movements and provides a climactic cap to all that has come before.

In his **Piano Sonata No. 30 in E, Op. 109,** Beethoven proves his outstanding ability to achieve the triumph of substance over form, of communication over technique. The ground plan for this three-movement sonata is audacious: it starts with a short first movement that alternates fast and slow sections as though combining the first and second movements. Even shorter in length, the high-speed second movement drives forward with unflagging energy. The first two movements function as an introduction to the third, an absolutely glorious theme and variations that is the climax of the piece. The result? One of the most extraordinary of all the Beethoven sonatas.

To enhance the contrast between the two themes of the first movement, Beethoven not only changes the key, melody, and character of the second theme, but he puts it in a completely different tempo. The first theme is a fast, light melody in a steady rhythm. The second assumes a very much slower, rhythmically freer character, considerably more serious and introspective than before. After considering only the opening theme in the development section, Beethoven returns both themes in their original tempos for the recapitulation and draws upon the first for the coda.

Possessed of a raging energy, the Prestissimo simply explodes into being. As strong as it is, though, the terse movement seemingly exists as a prelude to what is to follow.

Heard next is one of the most exquisite, exalted slow melodies that Beethoven ever invented. The composer then subjects this melody to six variations: the first superimposes a new melody on the original harmonies; the second sounds most like two variations in one—the first a bare outline of the theme in short, pointed notes, the second a more lyrical allusion to the beginning melody; the third variation is an exercise in counterpoint, the two voices independently speeding along, each involved with its own melodic line; the slower and warmer fourth variation goes far afield melodically while maintaining the essential harmonic structure; the fifth is an intricate contrapuntal variation; and the sixth starts with the primary theme, builds to a climax over a continuing trill, and ends with a simple, touching restatement of the original melody.

Completed on Christmas day, 1821, the **Piano Sonata No. 31 in A flat, Op. 110,** holds a special place as Beethoven's only composition dating from that year. In part it is because he was simultaneously working on his *Missa Solemnis* and Ninth Symphony and in part because he was sick, deaf, discouraged, lacking love and companionship, and beset by all sorts of family and financial difficulties. Nonetheless, the A-flat sonata proves to be a warm, glowing, personal statement, and it is probably the most frequently performed of the late sonatas.

Beethoven exercised particular care in including directions to the performer in this sonata. As an example, he marked the first-movement tempo Moderato cantabile, molto espressivo ("Moderate speed, songlike, with much expression"), but in case there was any doubt, he added the further words of guidance "con amabilità" ("sweetly, lovingly"). Without any powerful climaxes to interrupt the lyrical flow, the first movement is leisurely and

relaxed, tender and intimate. Although organized in sonata-allegro form, there are more than the typical two distinctive, contrasting themes. Rather, a great number of phrases interconnect
in a seemingly endless stream of melody without obscuring the
outline of the formal structure.

Usually performed with virtually no pause (as are all the subsequent movements) the scherzolike Allegro molto—fast, spirited, and with dramatic dynamic alternations—almost feels like
an intrusion, immediately smashing the mood that Beethoven
has so carefully established. A naive subsidiary theme follows; it
is believed to be an allusion to a popular Viennese street song of
the time, "Ich bin liederlich." The middle section, correspond-
ing to the trio of a scherzo, has the right hand busily scurrying
along with dynamic punctuations by left hand offbeats. A repeat
of the opening and a brief coda end this highly concentrated
movement.

The third and fourth movements can be considered one unit.
The slow third movement starts with an extended *recitative*—a
style of writing that is rhythmically and metrically free, based on
the flexible, natural patterns of human speech. At its conclusion
comes the Arioso dolente ("Sad song"), one of the most poignant, touching slow melodies of Beethoven's last period, sung
simply over an accompaniment of repeated chords. After the
Arioso fades away, Beethoven begins the crowning movement
of the sonata, the fugue.

Fugal writing—a form of polyphony or counterpoint in which
one melody is imitated in different voices—became very important to Beethoven in his final period. The last movement of Op.
110 provides one of the most accessible and satisfying examples
of this style of writing. The poised, dignified subject of the fugue
is of the utmost melodic and rhythmic simplicity, which is necessary in light of the increasing complexity that ensues as Beethoven builds the theme up into an elaborate three-voice fugue,
creating both a fascinating intellectual accomplishment and a
highly expressive emotional experience. After pursuing the
fugue for a while, Beethoven interrupts for a somewhat free
restatement of the Arioso section, which he asks to be played
"Ermattet klagend" ("Wearily complaining"). The movement

then picks up the fugue again—now marked *"Nach und nach wieder auflebend"* ("More and more gaining new life"). Here Beethoven puts the fugal subject through some astonishing transformations, including inverting the melody, shortening the note values (diminution), lengthening the note values (augmentation), and juxtaposing and altering the melody itself in various ways—all building to a stunning, concluding climax.

The **Piano Sonata No. 32 in C minor, Op. 111,** Beethoven's final piano sonata, was completed on January 13, 1822, just over five years before the composer's death. In a way, the Op. 111 serves as a summing up, a culmination, of the piano sonatas Beethoven had been writing for the previous twenty-six years. Op. 111 brings to their highest level three compositional styles and techniques that grew increasingly important in the composer's later sonatas: contrapuntal and fugal writing, the variation form, and the use of extended trills.

Analysis shows the organization of the first movement to be sonata-allegro form: a slow introduction, a stark, violent first theme, a second theme that is a brief moment of quiet respite in the midst of all the turbulence, a working-out section devoted entirely to the first theme, a very free restatement of both themes, and a short coda that softly fades away at the end. The texture throughout, however, is strongly contrapuntal. After the forceful unison statement of the principal theme scarcely a moment goes by without two or more independent lines of music being played and lines of melody being tossed about in fugal imitation.

The quiet ending of the first movement makes possible the huge expressive leap from that stormy, minor-key, worldly movement to the profoundly serene, major-key, spiritualistic second movement. Entitled Arietta ("Short Song"), it furnishes a perfectly fitting and satisfying conclusion to this sonata and to the amazing thirty-two piano sonatas that Beethoven wrote. Beethoven states a melody of transcendental simplicity and beauty and then subjects it to a number of variations in which the listener is transported out of the sphere of notes and fingers and keys to a remote and exalted realm. The first four variations are easily followed and understood. But then, as Beethoven introduces long, sustained trills, the sequence of carefully ordered variations dissolves. One senses that the theme is still growing, changing, evolving, but without being cast into individual variations. The theme, in close to its original form, makes its final appearance under a seemingly endless trill. And then all dissolves into silence.

Violin Sonatas

In a carryover from late-eighteenth-century practice, the ten Beethoven violin sonatas, like the cello sonatas, are designated for piano and violin, rather than the expected violin and piano. Nevertheless, the two instruments are essentially equal partners in the sonatas; neither voice is consistently subservient, neither one is overly dominant.

Beethoven composed nine of the ten violin sonatas from 1797 to 1803, from age twenty-seven to thirty-three. The first three, the **Sonatas for Piano and Violin, Op. 12, Nos. 1, 2, and 3,** consider well the needs of the amateur and dilettante—the primary consumers of such music. Although interpretatively and musically demanding, these early sonatas are well within the technical abilities of most serious amateurs; and their scope and dimensions place them more comfortably in an intimate salon or parlor than in a larger public concert hall. In the remaining seven sonatas Beethoven moves away from the *Hausmusik* character and toward a grander style more fit for professional performance in public recital.

The cheerful and genial Op. 12 sonatas already show Beethoven's sure hand in allowing the musical material to shape the structure and his ability to strike a perfect tonal balance between the very different instruments. Beethoven dedicated the sonatas to Antonio Salieri, his teacher for a short while after he arrived in Vienna; it is one of the rare instances where Beethoven inscribed a composition to a professional musician. These three sonatas are alike in a few respects: they are in three movements; the most serious and original music comes in the first movement; the slow movements, particularly in Numbers 2 and 3, are deeply emotional and expressive; and the finales sparkle with particular verve and optimism.

Originally the next two sonatas, composed in 1800 and 1801, were conceived as Op. 23, Nos. 1 and 2, but owing to an engraver's error were released separately as the **Sonata for Piano and Violin No. 4 in A minor, Op. 23,** and **Sonata for Piano and Violin No. 5 in F, Op. 24, "Spring."**

The fourth sonata, in the minor mode, has an underlying tension throughout. The first movement seethes with a powerful energy beneath the surface. By contrast, the slow movement, which is actually quite moderate in speed, projects a warm, comforting feeling. And the finale, spare and thin, moves forward with a strong, driving motion.

So fresh and charming is the F major sonata that it has acquired the nickname "Spring". After basking in the radiance of the opening movement, the listener is treated to a very simple, but highly emotional slow movement and a quirky Scherzo, in which the violin often finds itself one beat behind the piano. The sonata ends with a cheerful and bubbly finale.

Beethoven composed the three sonatas of Op. 30 for Czar Alexander I of Russia in 1802, although he was not paid for his labors until 1815, when the czar was attending the Congress of Vienna! The emotional focus of the **Sonata for Piano and Violin No. 6 in A, Op. 30, No. 1,** centers on the slow movement, the Adagio. It contains melodies and harmonies that could well have been composed by Verdi nearly a century later. While Beethoven originally wrote an exciting, breathtaking finale for the work, he later decided to substitute a gentle, lyrical, low-pressure theme and variations based on a Schubertian melody for that movement. (The composer later used the original finale as the last movement of the "Kreutzer" Sonata, Op. 47.)

The **Sonata for Piano and Violin No. 7 in C minor, Op. 30, No. 2,** ranks high among the Beethoven violin sonatas for its deeply felt emotional quality and the richness of its melodic invention. It is truly one of the most outstanding works in the violinist's repertoire. The composer wrote this sonata in C minor, a key he reserved for some of his most profound musical utterances, including the Fifth Symphony, Third Piano Concerto, and "Pathétique" Sonata. Dramatic and expressive, the first movement immediately sets a tone of tightly controlled intensity; it starts with the whip-crack opening and continues, almost without respite, to the end of the movement. After the relaxation of the Adagio cantabile, the Scherzo, which Beethoven had considered cutting, fairly crackles with rhythmic vitality. And the concluding Allegro very effectively continues the sonata's high level of electricity and excitement right through to the end.

The intensity and energy of the first movement of the **Sonata for Piano and Violin No. 8 in G, Op. 30, No. 3,** picks up where the C minor leaves off. Beethoven entitles the second movement Tempo di Minuetto, but the character is not especially dancelike; it resembles much more a tuneful, graceful intermezzo. The whirlwind finale can be considered a perpetual-motion movement; all the themes have a ceaseless flow of rapid notes, either as the leading or the subsidiary voice. The ongoing rush is stilled only for a brief moment in the coda before speeding on to the climactic conclusion.

Few musical compositions figure as prominently in an important work of fiction as the **Sonata for Piano and Violin No. 9 in A, Op. 47, "Kreutzer."** In Leo Tolstoy's novella *The Kreutzer Sonata,* it is the music of this composition that finally drives the jealous husband to murder his wife. The subtitle comes from the dedication to Rodolphe Kreutzer, the well-known French violinist and composer. Ironically enough, Berlioz let it be known in 1844 that Kreutzer "could never bring himself to play this outrageously unintelligible composition." The original dedication actually was intended for another famous violinist of the day, George Polgreen Bridgetower, but Beethoven struck out his name after a quarrel over a girl they both loved.

From Beethoven's journals we learn that he wrote the sonata in great haste, starting in March 1802, hoping that it would be ready in time for a concert he was giving with Bridgetower in Vienna on May 24. The pressure to finish was so enormous that for the last movement he recycled the discarded finale of an earlier violin sonata, Op. 30, No. 1, and at 4:30 A.M. on the morning of the concert he called on his student Ferdinand Ries to help copy out the violin part. Even so, Bridgetower still had to perform the second movement from the composer's nearly illegible manuscript, while Beethoven played the piano from sketches and his memory of what he had written in the final version.

On the title page of the "Kreutzer" Sonata Beethoven indicated that it was "composed in a very concertante style, somewhat like a concerto." Actually, the virtuosic piece has incredibly difficult parts for both players, making it in effect a double concerto for violin and piano *without* orchestra.

The "Kreutzer" has the distinction of being the longest of the ten violin sonatas and the only one with a slow introduction. The first movement, which hurtles along at a breakneck pace after the introduction, dazzles with its technically demanding parts, including many three- and four-note chords for the violin, cadenzalike interludes, and a number of breaks in the rhythm and changes in tempo.

After the feverish opening movement, the emotional temperature drops considerably for the Andante, a theme and variations. The first two variations focus on the jocular, playful nature of the theme itself. The third variation, written in the minor, conveys a rather more somber and contemplative character. Variation 4 is a paradigm of melodic decorations and ornaments, filled with sparkling trills and turns. The quiet and introspective coda that follows gives little hint of the gaiety in the early variations.

The sonata ends with a madly whirling dance based on the repeated long-short rhythmic pattern of the tarantella, an old Italian dance whose frenzied steps were once believed to be the result of the poisonous venom injected by the bite of the tarantula spider. The movement dashes to a tempestuous conclusion with scant time to catch a breath.

In the decade between the composition of the "Kreutzer" Sonata in 1802 and the completion of Beethoven's **Sonata for Piano and Violin No. 10 in G, Op. 96,** in 1812, his last violin sonata, the world changed considerably. Napoleon, the great hero of the early years of the century, had entered his decline, effectively bringing to an end the age of brave men and mighty nobles. The new world leaders, emerging from the middle class, were the bourgeoisie, the chief inheritors of society's wealth and power.

Beethoven's music reflected these changes in society. Where once his compositions were valiant and grandiose in character, they now became more modest and circumscribed, more in tune with the altered climate. His music began to show a new *Gemütlichkeit,* a warm, emotional attitude, with broadly sung melodies, moderate tempos, and appealing dance rhythms. In the G major sonata the warm glow of Beethoven's postheroic period emerges very clearly, as well as intimations of the greatness to come in his final works.

The first movement of the Op. 96 sonata maintains a simple, convivial outlook. The violin unceremoniously announces a sprightly little figure that Beethoven extends into the first theme. This is followed by a crisply rhythmic ascending melody that serves as the contrasting theme. From these two musical ideas Beethoven fashions a tender, gentle, and above all, appealing movement.

It is in the Adagio espressivo that we glimpse the sublime heights that late-period Beethoven can reach. The melodies smoothly pass back and forth between the instruments to create an exquisite, profoundly moving musical experience.

Following without pause, the Scherzo affords a release after the highly emotional slow movement. Although Beethoven seems to have been inspired by the newly emerging waltz, its oom-pah-pah rhythm never quite gets fully established because of the many offbeat accents that Beethoven persists in tossing about.

The last movement consists of a freely conceived theme and variations, though not so titled. The theme itself sounds like a simple, popular folksong. Beethoven puts the melody through all sorts of paces—lyrical, vigorous, somber, and gruff in turn. A slow variation, with long, much ornamented lines, interrupts before the tempo picks up and the movement rushes headlong to its powerful conclusion.

Alban Berg

Born February 9, 1885, in Vienna
Died December 24, 1935, in Vienna

THE leading artistic movement in Vienna in the early years of the twentieth century was Expressionism, an intensely personal, subjective, emotionally charged, highly romantic style that was overlaid with a sense of mystery and mysticism. The Expressionist movement grew from the particular mix of social and psychological beliefs and political and economic conditions in the German-speaking lands during that era. It was also, in part, a German and Austrian aesthetic reaction against Impressionism, the joyful and colorful artistic style that began in France in the latter part of the nineteenth century and was mostly concerned with fragmentary, fleeting glimpses of the surface appearance of reality. The Expressionist artists, on the other hand, strove to explore the unconscious, to probe the essence of their subjects, and to capture in their art, man's innermost thoughts and emotions.

Three composers, Alban Berg, along with his teacher Arnold Schoenberg and fellow student Anton Webern, were the leading exponents of Expressionism in music. Berg accepted as his own the credo enunciated by Gustav Klimt, the outstanding Expressionist painter: "To the age its art, to art its freedom." Although the musical realization of Expressionism was rooted in the compositions of Brahms, Wagner, Mahler, and Richard Strauss, the style of writing ventured far beyond these masters, advancing and pushing forward every element of music—melody, harmony, rhythm, and form.

Berg wrote only one sonata, his **Piano Sonata, Op. 1,** which he began in the summer of 1907 while still a student of Schoenberg. Both he and his teacher, however, considered this work a fully mature effort, and it was Schoenberg who suggested that Berg make the sonata his first published opus.

Although he originally planned it as a more traditional three-movement work, Berg had difficulty continuing after completing the extensive first movement. He was, therefore, only too willing to accept Schoenberg's recommendation that he end the sonata at that point.

Despite the advanced writing, the sonata follows a relatively standard overall sonata-allegro form. Berg builds up the intense and impassioned thematic material out of short fragments of dense melody that he presents with frequent changes of tempo. All of the themes, in both the main and subsidiary groups, derive from motifs heard in the first few bars. After the complex polyphonic exposition, the development section relaxes somewhat with a more homophonic texture. A varied and slightly lengthened recapitulation ends the movement. (Berg was obviously heeding Schoenberg's admonition to avoid literal repetitions; as Schoenberg said, "Never do what a copyist can do!")

The first performance of Berg's piano sonata, given in Vienna by Etta Werndorf, aroused the anger of the audience and the vitriol of the critics. Nonetheless, by now the work has won wide acceptance as a major twentieth-century contribution to the piano sonata literature.

Ernest Bloch

Born July 24, 1880, in Geneva
Died July 15, 1959, in Portland, Oregon

AFTER beginning violin lessons and starting to compose on his own, ten-year-old Ernest Bloch solemnly vowed that he would some day become a composer. He wrote out the pledge, placed the paper on a mound of stones, and burned it, symbolically setting the direction of his life's work. This dedication to music remained constant with him, and he, like many other composers of our time, always found the time to compose, even when he was forced to pursue such other activities as working in the family business in Geneva (1904–1916), teaching at the Mannes School in New York (1917–1920), founding and directing the Cleveland Institute of Music (1920–1925), directing the San Francisco Conservatory (1925–1930), and lecturing at the University of California, Berkeley (1940–1952).

Scholars often describe Bloch as a Neoromantic because of his extremely lush writing and the passion that pulsates through every measure. The most striking feature of Bloch's music, however, has to do with his close identification with the religious, cultural, and musical heritage of the Jewish people. "It is the Jewish soul that interests me," he once wrote, "the complex, glowing, agitated soul that I feel vibrating throughout the Bible." This overriding influence runs through all of his music, giving it a uniquely fervid quality and intensity.

A prolific composer, Bloch wrote in all forms—opera, symphony orchestra, chamber music, songs, and instrumental solos. Included are three sonatas, two for violin and piano and one for piano. The **Sonata No. 1 for Violin and Piano** came first, composed in 1920, the year Bloch arrived in Cleveland. The composer once described the piece very briefly, calling it a "tormented work . . . written soon after the terrible war and the terrible peace."

The first movement, although basically wild and savage in character, has some moments of luminous tranquillity to relieve the overall ferocity. The composer's directions, *Molto quieto* and *misterioso* ("Very quiet" and "mysteriously"), indicate the mood of the lovely cantilena second movement, which was inspired by a book about Tibet that Bloch was reading at the time. Written as a barbaric march, the powerful third movement exploits the resources of the piano as a percussive instrument.

The story behind the creation of the **Sonata No. 2 for Violin and Piano, "Poème mystique,"** bears retelling. At a performance of his first violin sonata, Bloch sensed that the audience was having a difficult time comprehending and accepting the music's violence and anguish. This perception led him to contemplate composing a tranquil, optimistic work for the same instruments. But it was a dream that he had in 1924, following a very serious illness, that provided the actual inspiration and started him composing. Written in one continuous movement, the sonata combines the inflections of ancient Hebraic psalms with excerpts from the Credo and Gloria as sung in the Catholic liturgy.

The 1935 **Piano Sonata,** which was written in a little hamlet in the Swiss-Italian Alps, consists of three movements performed without interruption. Bloch described the first movement as having "an obscure and metallic character without a trace of sentimentalism." Using as a transition an echo of the introduction, a passage of ascending and descending broken chords, Bloch moves directly to the second movement. This Pastorale evokes, in the composer's words, "the peace and majesty of mountains far from the conflict and struggles of life." The last movement depicts an ancient Chinese sculpture, *God of War,* which shows an ugly creature trampling on its hapless victims. After building to an overwhelming climax, the music quiets down and ends with a lengthy coda—Bloch called it "obscure and mysterious"—that contains quotes from all three movements.

Johannes Brahms

Born May 7, 1833, in Hamburg
Died April 3, 1897, in Vienna

"BACH, Beethoven, and Brahms" is a well-known alliteration attributed to the pianist and conductor Hans von Bülow, a friend of Brahms's. Very likely Brahms heard this expression and was well aware of the musical mantle he had inherited from his predecessors. In fact, he commented that one of the two most important events in his lifetime was the publication of the collected works of Bach, begun in 1850. (The other was Bismarck's unification of Germany in 1871.) At another time he wrote, "You do not know what it is like, hearing [Beethoven's] footsteps constantly behind me." Briefly put, from Beethoven, Brahms acquired his monumental architectonic sense and his use of brief motifs that allow for expansive development; from Bach, he drew his feeling for polyphony.

To these major influences must be added Brahms's affection for ethnic music, which can be heard in his many settings and quotations of folk melodies and his creation of original themes with a folk-music quality. And finally, despite his affinity for the music of Bach and Beethoven, he was able to infuse all of his compositions with the passion and powerful personal emotions that characterize nineteenth-century Romantic music.

Cello Sonatas

Some commentators hear in Brahms's **Sonata for Piano and Cello No. 1 in E minor, Op. 38,** the composer's homage to his distinguished forebears. In addition to the general tone and approach, his obeisance to Bach appears in the main themes of the first and third movements, which bear some resemblance to Contrapunctus 3 and Contrapunctus 13, respectively, of Bach's monumental *Art of the Fugue.* In addition, Brahms wrote the third movement as a fugue, a form closely identified with Bach, but also associated with Beethoven, since the last movement of Beethoven's fifth cello sonata (Op. 102, No. 2), is also fugal. Designating the sonatas as for piano and cello, rather than for cello and piano, further evidences Brahms's deference to earlier practices.

The principal theme of the first movement, a beautifully crafted creation, projects a noble, restrained dignity and is organized into a gentle arch shape. Yet in the course of working out this melody, Brahms transforms the turning point, where the ascending line changes direction, into a highly emotional outcry.

Although Brahms calls the second movement Allegretto quasi Menuetto ("Somewhat fast, in the style of a Minuet") its poignant, somewhat whimsical character shows little affinity for that old dance form. Perhaps Valse triste, as suggested by Brahms's biographer Karl Geiringer, would have been more apt. In any case, it is a movement of great beauty and appeal, starting with a little turn of melody in the piano that provides the impetus for all the following themes—dainty and decorous in the opening and closing sections, more lyrical in the middle.

The tender, docile mood of the first two movements is shattered by the energetic downward leap in the piano that ushers in the fugal subject of the finale. By writing a thick, complex piano part, which requires that the cellist play with great strength and power just to be heard, Brahms places virtuosic demands on the two performers. This despite the fact that in a letter to his publisher, Brahms wrote that the sonata "is undifficult to play for both instruments."

(Brahms first wrote three movements of the Op. 38 sonata in 1862, but omitted a finale. In June 1865 he composed a new concluding movement and dropped the second, an Adagio, producing the present three-movement work.)

A full twenty-one years passed before Brahms composed his

Sonata for Piano and Cello No. 2 in F, Op. 99, in August 1886. The composer was now fifty-three years old. While one hears in some of his works from the late 1880s, despite their great beauty and expressivity, a slightly lower energy level, there is no hint in the F major sonata that Brahms's powers were waning. The F major sonata is a strong, vigorous work, spacious in conception, and demanding in its instrumental writing.

The first movement evokes the setting where Brahms wrote the sonata—the shore of Lake Thun in Switzerland among the soaring Alps. The principal theme leaps about with great vitality, perhaps a musical analogue to the jagged peaks of the Swiss landscape and the jumping steps of the mountain folk dances. The overall youthful ardor and passion grow even more intense with the frequent use of tremolos—rapid alternation of notes— particularly for the piano, but for the cello as well. The density of the writing probably influenced Brahms to keep the cello high in its range so it could be heard over the piano.

Brahms showed that he was eager to place the second movement at a remove from the others by directing that it be played Adagio, a very slow tempo in the midst of three Allegro movements, and placing it in the distant key of F-sharp major, with the others in F major. The movement opens most dramatically with the cello playing pizzicato, creating an atmosphere of fear and foreboding, while the remainder of the heart-on-the-sleeve movement seems much more consoling, as well as highly emotional.

The turbulence and agitation of the first movement return for the following Allegro passionato. In clearly delineated three-part form, the movement opens with a thrusting, thundering section that gives way to a more lyrical, though intense, middle part, before ushering in a shortened reprise of the first section.

After the pressure and drive of the first three movements, the finale offers a respite of insouciant charm and relaxation. Cast in rondo form, Brahms furnishes several contrasting episodes between statements of the theme, an ingenuous folklike melody.

Clarinet Sonatas

When Brahms submitted the manuscript of his G major string quintet to the publisher in December 1890, he enclosed a note saying, "With this letter you can bid farewell to my music—because it is certainly time to leave off." At about the same time, his close friend Dr. Theodore Billroth commented, "He rejected the idea that he . . . would ever compose anything."

Then, in March 1891, on a visit to Meiningen, Brahms heard a performance by Richard Mühlfeld, principal clarinetist of the ducal orchestra. So captivated was the composer by Mühlfeld, whom he called the greatest wind player alive, that he again took up his pen and over the next few years wrote for Mühlfeld a clarinet trio, a clarinet quintet, and two clarinet sonatas.

The opening movement of the **Sonata for Clarinet and Piano in F minor, Op. 120, No. 1,** marked Allegro appassionato, immediately puts the lie to any thought that Brahms's fire and passion were spent. Between its surging, fervid first theme and its rhythmically quirky second theme, the music almost never relaxes until the slightly slower coda brings the music to a calm, reflective close.

Delicate and ethereal, the second movement provides a sharp contrast to what came before. The clarinet sings its thin, pure melodic line while the piano supplies an almost skeletal accompaniment. Brahms enriches the texture a bit when he introduces the subsidiary subject, but he maintains an overall delicacy of sound as he briefly develops the two themes and brings them back for a slightly varied recapitulation.

A gentle serenity pervades the Allegretto grazioso. The first part moves along with the rhythmic lilt of a ländler, the precursor of the waltz. In the middle section, Brahms exploits the exotic sound of the clarinet in its lowest register. The movement ends with a return of the opening.

Like a bright ray of sunshine, the Vivace bursts forth with great intensity. Structured as a rondo, the principal subject contains a number of separate motifs, starting with an arresting repeated three-note figure.

Brahms opens the **Sonata for Clarinet and Piano in E flat,**

Op. 120, No. 2, with a long, suave melodic line spun out by the clarinet while the piano carries on a flowing accompaniment. After quickly building to a climax, Brahms introduces the second theme, which seems static and immobile following the sweep of the first theme. After working through the two themes, Brahms ends the movement with a slow coda in which duplets (two notes to a beat) in the piano are played against triplets (three notes to a beat) in the clarinet.

Not fast and light enough to be a scherzo and too intense and important for an intermezzo, the second movement is a unique— and very special—creation. The fiery, ardent opening and closing sections contrast splendidly with the more stolid central part.

The concluding Andante con moto contains a theme and six variations. For the first three variations, Brahms uses successively shorter note values. The remaining three variations go much further afield, until the movement ends with a sparkling exhibition of cross-rhythms and virtuosic display.

After composing the two sonatas of Op. 120 in 1894 for clarinet and piano, Brahms transcribed them for viola and piano; they now play an equally important part in the repertoire of both instruments.

Piano Sonatas

Brahms wrote his three piano sonatas over the period of just one year, beginning in November 1852 when he was only nineteen years old. Though early works, these sonatas already show the composer to be a most able explorer of new sonorities for the piano and a master of formal organization.

Perhaps the most striking feature of all three sonatas is their flamboyant romanticism. Coruscating through their pages is a passion, excitement, and power that bespeak a creator very much in tune with the exuberance and freedom of the Romantic revolution. Beneath this wild abandon, though, and providing a clue to his future development, are the set structures Brahms inherited from his Classical forefathers.

The **Piano Sonata No. 1 in C, Op. 1,** was the first work that Brahms, perhaps the most critical and self-demanding of all com-

posers, allowed to be published. He completed three movements—the first, third and fourth—in January 1853, having finished the second movement, an Andante, the previous year. On
the title page he wrote "Fourth Sonata," indicating that he had
already written three—one later published as Op. 2 and two
others that he discarded.

When Hans von Bülow dubbed Brahms's Symphony No. 1
"Beethoven's Tenth," he should have also named Brahms's first
piano sonata "Beethoven's Thirty-third." The overall vitality,
the strict organization, the palpable tension developed in each
movement, all evidence a spiritual affinity to the older master.
Also the very strong resemblance of the opening of the sonata to
the opening of Beethoven's *"Hammerklavier"* Sonata (which
Brahms heard many times) attests even more specifically to the
young man's devotion to his great predecessor.

Two of the movements show extramusical connections: the
second movement consists of three free variations on an old German *Minnelied,* "Verstohlen geht der Mond auf," a quiet, simple
love song. The finale takes its inspiration from Robert Burns's
poem "My Heart's in the Highlands." The music also abounds
with melodic cross-references, the best examples being the allusions to the opening theme that occur in the main subjects of the
third and fourth movements.

Although written earlier, in November 1852, Brahms published the **Piano Sonata No. 2 in F-sharp minor, Op. 2,** after
the C major. This older work fairly bursts with sections of Romantic excess that fit very comfortably and naturally between
sections of great intimacy. As in the first sonata, there are melodic interrelationships between the movements, and the slow
movement is a set of variations based on an old German folksong, "Mir ist Leide."

By far the most popular of the three sonatas, the **Piano Sonata
No. 3 in F minor, Op. 5,** projects a feeling of impressive drama
and great dynamic intensity. The sonata contains five movements, like the older forms of the suite and divertimento, but
they were not all written at the same time. Brahms composed the
two slow (even-numbered) movements first and then wrote the
three fast movements in October 1853.

Brahms presents the stunning opening phrase of the sonata in many variants and guises throughout the first movement, although the basic organization follows sonata-allegro form. The energy level remains high throughout, projecting a powerful quality of concentration and compression as the movement unfolds.

Brahms inscribed a short poem, by Otto Sternau (pseudonym of A. Inkermann), before the Andante espressivo. The nocturnal quality of the music successfully captures the tender emotions of the two lovers.

> *Der Abend dämmert*
> *Das Mondlicht scheint*
> *Da sind zwei Herzen*
> *In Liebe vereint*
> *Und halten sich selig umfangen* . . .

> The evening is falling
> The moonbeams rise
> And light two lovers
> Who mingle their sighs
> And commune in happiness together . . .

The following Scherzo provides an effective contrast; its sections of verve and energy alternate with moments of quiet and tranquillity.

The Intermezzo, which Brahms marked *"Rückblick"* ("Reminiscence"), supplies an affectionate reminder of the Andante espressivo.

Adapting an approach much favored by Beethoven, Brahms ends his musical journey on an affirmative, triumphant note. Following the organization of a free rondo, the last movement sprinkles several references to previously heard melodies in this exultant conclusion.

One suspects that Brahms set himself a number of expressive and technical goals to meet in his piano sonatas. Perhaps with the Op. 5 he felt he had achieved these objectives, because he did not return to the form during the remaining forty-four years of his life.

Violin Sonatas

The **Sonata for Piano and Violin No. 1 in G, Op. 78,** sometimes bears the nickname *"Regenlied"* ("Rain Song"). The subtitle derives from the fact that the theme of Brahms's song of that name figures prominently in the last movement of the sonata and its particular rhythm (almost trochaic, with three repeated notes in the pattern of note, pause, short note, long note) recurs throughout the work. The song calls out to the rain to reawaken childhood dreams and to recollect once again songs from the past.

It is hard to know whether Brahms borrowed from "Regenlied" for the sake of its melody alone or for the purpose of expressing the meaning of the song in instrumental terms. What is known, though, is that Brahms wrote Otto Dessoff, the prominent conductor, "You must not complain about the rain. It can be set very well to music, something I have tried to do along with spring in a violin sonata."

Brahms began making sketches for the first violin sonata in 1878, completing the composition in the summer of 1879 while at the resort of Portschach-am-See. Although it is Brahms's first published violin sonata, it is actually the fourth one he wrote, since he destroyed three earlier attempts. The overall character of the music is Apollonian, projecting gentle serenity and restraint more than fire and fury, even though the music does, on occasion, rise to high points of excitement.

The sonata opens with the immediate violin presentation of the *Regenlied* rhythm over simple reiterated chords in the piano. As the theme is extended, the piano begins a rapid figuration that appears here and in the following movements, evoking the pattering sound of falling raindrops. Brahms also gives the violin the responsibility for introducing the second theme, a rich, lyrical melody that alludes to the *Regenlied* rhythm.

The opening of the Adagio bears no resemblance to the *Regenlied* pattern; but the slightly faster middle section centers around a variant of the all-important rhythmic gesture.

In the finale, the *Regenlied* motif comes to fruition as the principal theme of the rondo-form movement; it presents itself three times, with contrasting interludes. Of especial interest is the second interlude, which is the main subject of the previous Adagio. When the movement, and sonata, come to a quiet close, it is not on a note of despair, but with an attitude of calm optimism.

Brahms rarely hesitated to joke about his music and to deprecate his composing efforts. In a letter to his publisher, Simrock, Brahms asked if he could be sued for borrowing from his own songs, as in the G major sonata. Moreover, the composer humorously offered to waive twenty-five percent of his usual fee since the sonata only contained three movements. Sometime later, when presenting the manuscript of the sonata to the wife of Miller zu Aichholz, his covering letter mentioned that it was written on "stronger paper in which to pack birthday presents."

The **Sonata for Piano and Violin No. 2 in A, Op. 100,** has two rarely used subtitles: "Die Meistersinger," because the first three notes of the work happen to be the same as the opening of Walther's "Prize Song" in Wagner's opera; the "Thun" sonata, because it was composed near Lake Thun in Switzerland during the summer of 1886 and Brahms's host, Joseph Viktor Widmann, wrote a flowery poem about the music, "Thunersonate von Johannes Brahms."

The radiant music of the A major sonata is suffused with glowing intimacy, sweetness, and gentility. As Elizabeth von Herzogenberg, a former student and trusted friend of Brahms, put it, "The whole sonata is a caress." In describing the music, Brahms said a number of his songs "go into the sonata." For example, the opening melody quotes from his song "Komm bald." Following this comes the tune of "Wie Melodien zieht es mir" that serves as the second theme. And in the finale fleeting references are made to several songs—"Immer leiser wird mein Schlummer," "Auf dem Kirchhofe," "Meine Liede," and "Meine liebe ist grün." Even though the first theme dominates, the opening movement seems to take its character mostly from the subsidiary theme source, "Wie Melodien," the text of which compares love to an elusive melody or the scent of flowers.

The Andante tranquillo combines a slow movement and a scherzo by alternating slow, lyrical sections with lively dancelike interludes. And the last movement, more contemplative than the others, makes excellent use of the dark, rich sonorities that can be elicited from the violin's lowest string, the G string.

In some ways the **Sonata for Piano and Violin No. 3 in D minor, Op. 108,** written during the summer of 1888 at Thun, Switzerland, is the apotheosis of Brahms's three sonatas. Not only does it retain some of the special features of the earlier works—the song quotations (the principal theme of the Adagio is from "Klage"), but it goes far beyond the previous sonatas in scope and scale, in dramatic sweep, and in virtuosic demands on both players. The concentrated power, virility, and sureness of the work moved Clara Schumann to write to Brahms, "What a wonderfully beautiful thing you have once more given us."

With the statement of the main subject, Brahms immediately puts us on notice that this is indeed a distinctive work. Although marked *sotto voce* (literally "under the voice," or "under the breath"), the glorious, soaring opening theme as played by the two instruments creates the sensation of limitless space and of compelling sweep and urgency. Brahms introduces a more earthbound melody with the second subject, providing an effective counterfoil to the earlier ethereal theme. After building to some impassioned moments as he develops and returns the two themes, Brahms finally allows the music to quietly fade away.

The Adagio can be considered the emotional fulcrum of the sonata. Although simple in conception and design, it is nonetheless a deeply felt and profoundly moving musical utterance.

Of the third movement, Clara Schumann said that it is "like a beautiful girl frolicking with her lover—then suddenly, in the middle of it all, a flash of deep passion, only to make way for sweet dalliance once more." Brahms accomplishes all this with but one theme—a pert, rhythmic phrase introduced by the piano —that he transforms and intensifies for the impassioned middle section.

The finale unfolds as the biggest movement of the sonata, filled with fiery conflict and fevered emotion. This spirited section pushes both instruments to the limits of their sound production, achieving effects that are almost symphonic in impact.

Frédéric Chopin

Born February 22, 1810, in Zelazowa Wola, Poland
Died October 17, 1849, in Paris

ANY study of Chopin's music soon reveals the striking centrality of the piano in all of his compositions, from the many works for solo piano, to the two concerti for piano and orchestra, to the several works for piano plus one or two instruments or voice. In fact, his unique style of piano writing was so perfectly suited for the instrument that it became the dominant influence on keyboard writing for the remainder of the nineteenth century. His was a special ability to create melodies and harmonies that showed off the piano to its best advantage, made the instrument exceptionally expressive and emotional, and at all times maintained an elegance and refinement without any overt virtuosic display for its own sake.

One musical device that Chopin employed to great advantage is rubato ("robbed" in Italian), a flexible, elastic performance style that intentionally speeds up some notes and holds back others, avoiding a strict metronomic tempo or rhythm. Every piece that Chopin wrote should be played with rubato. But because there is no practical way to notate rubato, it is up to the interpreter's skill and sensitivity to determine the exact amount of liberty that should be taken with the printed notes.

Since Chopin habitually said and wrote little about his music, many details about his compositions are lacking. It is known, however, that his usual approach to a new work was to start improvising at the keyboard. As soon as he came up with a particularly pleasing idea, he would work very hard to give it shape

and realize its full potential. Although his music is highly romantic and expressive, Chopin never associated any of his works with
programmatic, extramusical ideas. Any meanings beyond the
music itself are left to the imagination of the performer and
listener.

Chopin wrote four sonatas—three for solo piano and one for
cello and piano. The formal organization he employed in all of
these sonatas is the same. The first movement is moderately fast
in tempo (only the Piano Sonata No. 2 has a slow introduction)
and in sonata-allegro form, with an exposition that presents two
contrasting themes, a development of one or both themes, and a
return of one or both themes in the recapitulation. The second
serves as the dance movement—a minuet in the first piano sonata, a faster, lighter scherzo in all the others. The slow movement always comes next. And all the sonatas end with a very fast
movement.

The **Piano Sonata No. 1 in C minor, Op. 4,** the earliest of
Chopin's sonatas, was composed in 1827 and perhaps early
1828, while he was still a pupil of Joseph Elsner at the Warsaw
Conservatory. As a student work it is, perhaps, of greater historical than musical value. The finest movement is the third, an
exquisite Larghetto in highly unconventional five-beat time, one
of the earliest examples of this rarely used meter.

The **Piano Sonata No. 2 in B-flat minor, Op. 35, "Funeral
March,"** ranks above all the Chopin sonatas in terms of popularity and frequency of performance. In fact, one can hardly hear
this sonata without reacting emotionally to the third movement,
the familiar Marche funèbre. The melody, which has become a
popular cliché evocative of death and funerals, sounds so familiar
that its associative message is often more powerful than its musical communication.

Chopin wrote the Funeral March movement first, in 1837,
finishing the remaining three movements of the sonata a full two
years later, during the first summer he spent with his lover, nov-
elist George Sand (Aurore Dudevant), at her country home in
Nohant, near Paris. Although many feel that the piece is well
integrated, some say that the two-year gap during its creation
and Chopin's difficulty in conceiving large-scale works are re-

sponsible for movements that vary too much in style and character and lack the necessary unity for an artistically satisfying sonata. Robert Schumann was of this opinion. "The idea of calling it a sonata," he wrote, "is a caprice, if not a jest, for [Chopin] has simply bound together four of his wildest children, perhaps in order to smuggle them under this name into a place where they otherwise might not fit."

After a few introductory measures, Chopin presents the two themes of the opening movement, the first agitated, with a somewhat tragic mien, the second more relaxed and consoling. The development deals exclusively with the first theme so that Chopin brings back the second theme only in the recapitulation.

Like the opening movement, the Scherzo starts under a cloud of unease and nervous anxiety. The middle section, the Trio, proffers a contrast with a poised, elegant vocal melodic line, before the initial turmoil returns. A final glimpse of the Scherzo ends the movement.

The Marche funèbre begins with the oppressive gloom of the well-known melody. A change of mood to somewhat greater optimism follows, but before long it gives way once again to the despair of the grief-laden opening march.

Where can Chopin go after the black darkness of the Marche funèbre? Offering neither solace nor confirmation of doom, Chopin concludes the sonata with a fast, strikingly short (just over one minute) movement in which the two hands double in octaves, playing a musical line that seems to lack distinctive melodic shape, rhythmic pattern, and tonal center. Chopin once offered this perhaps ironic explanation: "The left hand in unison with the right hand is gossiping after the funeral." To the nineteenth-century composer and pianist Anton Rubinstein, the last movement sounded like "night winds sweeping over the churchyard graves."

In 1844, during his last happy summer with George Sand at Nohant, Chopin wrote his **Piano Sonata No. 3 in B minor, Op. 58.** Bold and forceful, this work finds the composer in peak form, and far more positive in outlook. After an almost playful opening melody, Chopin introduces an absolutely charming, flowing, lyrical second subject. As in the second sonata, the composer spends so much time with the first theme in the development that he does not deem it necessary to bring that melody back in the recapitulation.

The Scherzo is a creation of Chopin at his quicksilver, sparkling best. After the glistening opening, the composer provides the perfect foil, an interlude with a straightforward, simple melody. The movement ends with a shortened reprise of the first part.

The Largo brings to mind the style and character of one of Chopin's graceful and evocative nocturnes. This slow movement creates the same languid, melancholy ambiance he fashions so effectively in his shorter character pieces.

The Finale opens in a burst of energy that sends the pianist clambering all over the keyboard. The vigorous theme that follows shoots forward with powerful rhythmic propulsion. Spiced with some brilliant passagework, the movement rises to ever higher levels of excitement as it drives on.

The years following the writing of the B minor sonata were difficult ones for Chopin as his relationship with George Sand grew more and more strained, resulting finally in their separation in 1847. During those trying times Chopin wrote his **Sonata for Cello and Piano in G minor, Op. 65,** which proved to be Chopin's last major composition. The composer was helped in the writing by his good friend, cellist Auguste Franchomme, who advised Chopin on how to write idiomatically for the instrument.

The sonata starts with a piano statement of the leading theme, seemingly to confirm the expectation that Chopin could not resist giving the piano an advantage over the cello. But the cello soon interrupts for a more thorough traversal of the same melody. And for the remainder of the sonata the two instruments are comfortably balanced, with the two parts of equal importance and both proving to be quite difficult and demanding for the performers.

At first opinions were divided on the quality of the first movement. Some of Chopin's friends convinced him that it was obscure and contained too many ideas, so that at the premiere (Paris, February 2, 1848, Franchomme and Chopin) he programmed only the last three movements. Many later commentators found the movement perfectly fine, including Donald Francis Tovey, the famed English writer on musical subjects, who called it "masterly and terse," and it is now unquestioningly accepted as part of the sonata.

The Scherzo makes use of short motifs that Chopin treats sequentially, repeating essentially the same melodic figures, but starting each one on a different note. The middle section, with its elegant writing for the cello, gives the impression that the instrument is second only to the piano in Chopin's affection.

In true egalitarian spirit, the Largo passes the lovely theme and its various extensions and expansions back and forth fairly between the cello and piano.

The finale sounds like a cross between a rondo and a sonata-allegro movement. The dominant theme includes little slithering chromatic runs set within its overall vaulting athletic character. The major contrasting theme has a distinctive charm that gains from the insouciant afterbeats in the piano.

Muzio Clementi

Born January 23, 1752, in Rome
Died March 10, 1832, in Evesham, England

IN the course of Muzio Clementi's rich and long life, he achieved international success as a composer, pianist, music publisher, and manufacturer of pianos. Two remarkable, though unrelated, incidents give some indication of his special talents: In 1766 a wealthy Englishman, Peter Beckford, heard Clementi play the piano and, in effect, convinced his father to sell his fourteen-year-old son as an indentured servant for a period of seven years, during which time his main obligation would be to provide music at Beckford's country house. Some years later, in December 1781, while on tour in Vienna, Clementi was pitted against Mozart in a piano-playing and improvising contest—and the outcome was adjudged a draw!

His later years were likewise distinguished, but in quite a different way. In 1803, at age fifty-one, Clementi married an eighteen-year-old woman who bore him a son, but she died in childbirth. Eight years later, when he was fifty-nine years old, he took a twenty-six-year-old bride, who gave him, over the following years, four more children.

Between 1770 and 1821 Clementi found time to compose an impressive number of piano sonatas—anywhere from sixty to eighty, depending on which expert's opinion you accept. These sonatas constitute the central core of his compositional efforts.

Clementi considered the sonata a form for serious musical discourse and expression. His many piano sonatas adopt a virtuosic approach to the instrument, express great emotion, and seem to favor thick textures and sonorous chords. Their importance comes from the vital role they played in helping to establish a style of writing for the recently accepted piano and in setting the formal structure of the keyboard sonata. Only a few of his compositions, though, attain the high musical quality found in comparable works by such contemporaries as Haydn, Mozart, and Beethoven and these are the ones that have won places on modern recital programs.

While Clementi experimented with two-movement schemes in his earlier works, almost all of his later sonatas contain three movements. In the majority of these sonatas, the first movement is in sonata-allegro form, the themes being built up from short motifs, with the second subject sometimes derived from the first. Slow in tempo, the second movement takes on a lyrical and songlike character. The greatest display of verve and energy is reserved for the last movement, which is fast and cast either in rondo or sonata-allegro form.

The brilliant **Piano Sonata in B flat, Op. 25, No. 3,** is a popular favorite and was often programmed by Vladimir Horowitz. The **Piano Sonata in B minor, Op. 40, No. 2,** in two movements that are highly reminiscent of Beethoven's style, also rates high among Clementi's works.

The distinguished pianist and conductor Rudolph Ganz considered the **Piano Sonata in B flat, Op. 47, No. 2, "Magic Flute,"** to be Clementi's finest composition. The theme of the first movement became, ten years later, the main melody of Mozart's Overture to *The Magic Flute.*

The final sonata, the **Piano Sonata in G minor, Op. 50, No. 3,** *"Didone abbandonata,"* stands out as Clementi's only programmatic composition. The sonata, which the composer further described as "Scena tragica," focuses on a musical depiction of the Dido and Aeneas legend. It has but one main melody, which Clementi brings back many times, changing and varying it for each appearance—a technique that later came to be known as "thematic transformation" and was much used by Franz Liszt.

Aaron Copland

Born November 14, 1900, in Brooklyn, New York

PROBABLY no composer is more often identified as the voice of modern American music than Aaron Copland. His dance scores, such as *Billy the Kid, Rodeo,* and *Appalachian Spring,* are accepted classics. His orchestral compositions, including *El Salón México* and *Lincoln Portrait,* are popular favorites. And the rest of his considerable output of operas, chamber works, songs, choral pieces, and scores for stage, films, and television has put him in the forefront of twentieth-century composers.

In 1935 Copland began preparing sketches for his **Piano Sonata,** but dropped the project until January 1939 when the American playwright Clifford Odets offered the composer a commission to complete the work. Copland estimated that it would take two months; he finished twenty months later, on September 25, 1941, in Santiago, Chile, while on a State Department–sponsored goodwill tour of South America. Shortly thereafter, on October 21, Copland gave the premiere in Buenos Aires.

The music that Copland was composing around the time of the Piano Sonata could be categorized as public music, designed to be easily understood and enjoyed by large audiences. Unlike his other works of this period, the sonata emerges completely uncompromising and highly personal; as Copland said, "It is a serious piece that requires careful and repeated study." While many consider it harsh and highly discordant, Copland takes exception to this view. He has said, "There is considerable dissonance in it, yet the work is predominantly consonant."

In his autobiography, *Copland* (written with Vivian Perlis), the composer includes brief descriptions of each of the movements of the sonata. "The first movement," he writes, "is a regular sonata allegro form with two themes, a development section characterized by disjunct rhythms and a playful mood, and a clear recapitulation in which the opening idea is dramatically restated." The initial theme consists of two motifs—a progression of stark, dissonant chords and a five-note motif played deep in the bass. The second theme derives from the descending interval at the start of the first theme.

"The second-movement scherzo is rhythmically American—I never would have thought of those rhythms if I had not been familiar with jazz." Structured in three parts, the scherzo includes a light, mercurial opening and closing and a middle section that maintains the same essential character.

"The third movement of the Sonata is free in form and further from the classic sonata than the previous movements." With its echoes of melodies from earlier movements, the slow finale has the effect of releasing and resolving the tensions built up in the movements that came before.

Copland began his **Sonata for Violin and Piano** in 1942 in Oakland, New Jersey, and completed it the following year in Hollywood, where he was composing the score to the film *North Star.* In describing the sonata the composer said, "There are no complexities—it's an uncomplicated and direct statement of rather uncomplicated and direct musical ideas that I enjoyed developing. Above all, the work is lyrical and emphasizes the singing qualities of the violin. There is little pretense to virtuosity." Spirituality and calm pervade the piece, with a mood that is in part elegiac and in part pastoral in the first two movements, and touched by jazz in the finale. Overall, it is an appealing, attractive piece, despite a certain spare and dry writing style.

"The first movement alternates in mood between a tender lyricism and more rapid-paced sections," writes Copland. Moderate in tempo, the movement opens with solemn piano chords that bring to mind an austere New England church service.

Above this the violin introduces the five-note motif that is the germ cell from which the entire movement grows.

"The slow movement is bare in outline and poetic in nature. Harmonically it is very plain—'white notey,' you might say." Over the piano's slowly rising and falling scale line, the violin gives out a melody that sounds like the *cantus firmus* from an old church hymn. The texture throughout remains sparse and thin. A point of interest is the recall of the motif from the opening movement.

"The last movement is . . . snappy and rather rhythmically intricate, combining light and bouncy material with sections that are more serious in tone." Following the second movement without pause, the finale structure follows free rondo form in which the principal subject occurs three times, and the two contrasting interludes are drawn from the melody heard at the outset.

Copland dedicated the Violin Sonata to his friend, Lieutenant Harry H. Dunham, who was killed in World War II. With the violinist Ruth Posselt, Copland gave the first performance in New York on January 17, 1944.

Arcangelo Corelli

Born February 17, 1653, in Fusignano, Italy
Died January 8, 1713, in Rome

ARCANGELO CORELLI, who was equally renowned as a violinist
and composer and who, through these endeavors, helped to establish the basis for the modern school of violin playing, and
Antonio Stradivarius (1644–1737), who set the accepted standard of excellence in violin making, made the latter years of the
seventeenth century truly a golden age for the violin.

Corelli spent almost his entire professional life in Rome,
mostly residing in the palace of music-loving Cardinal Pietro
Ottoboni, where the composer presented weekly Monday eve-
ning concerts that were considered the most important events in
Rome's musical life. His published output, which is comparatively limited in quantity, is confined to sonatas and concertos,
and always features the violin. Corelli produced a total of six
opus numbers, each containing twelve individual compositions.
Opp. 1, 2, 3, and 4 are trio sonatas for two violins, harpsichord,
and cello; Op. 5 is sonatas for violin and harpsichord; and Op. 6
is concerti grossi for orchestra.

The full title of the Op. 5 violin and harpsichord sonatas is **12
Sonatas for Violin and Bass or Harpsichord, Op. 5.** Corelli
wrote two separate lines of music for each sonata—one for the
violin and one for the bass line, called figured bass *(basso continuo)* or thoroughbass. The bass line includes numbers or figures beneath the notes that indicate to the harpsichord player the
chords and harmonies that should be played in "realizing" the
figured bass part. (Most modern editions have the full harp-

sichord part written out as realized by the editors, since today's players are not as adept at playing from a figured bass line as were the harpsichordists in Corelli's day.)

Some scholars believe that the music is enhanced by having a third musician, usually playing a cello or viola da gamba, doubling the bass line along with the left hand of the harpsichord. While violin and harpsichord, with or without the extra bass instrument, come closest to Corelli's concept of how the music should sound, the sonatas may certainly be played with piano if that is the only keyboard instrument available.

The first six sonatas of Op. 5 are of the type known as *sonata da chiesa* ("church sonata"); they tend to be serious works, suitable for performance in church. Corelli's church sonatas consist of five movements, organized by tempo either as Slow, Fast, Fast, Slow, Fast, or as Slow, Fast, Slow, Fast, Fast. When there are two consecutive fast movements, Corelli avoids monotony by making the first fugal, with one voice imitating the other, and the second homophonic, or accompanied melody.

Much more varied are the last six sonatas of the opus; five of them are of the *sonata da camera* ("chamber sonata") type. Somewhat lighter in style, each begins with a Preludio and then goes on to three or four additional movements in the style and rhythm of such dances as the Giga, Gavotta, Sarabanda, Allemanda, and Corrente. As with the church sonatas, basically they alternate slow and fast movements. The differing rhythmic patterns keep the music colorful and interesting, even when one fast movement follows another.

Most commentators seem to agree that, in general, the slow movements of the sonatas are the more inspired sections; they gracefully combine great ease and flow with deep expressivity. If the violin parts are performed exactly as Corelli wrote them, however, these slow-moving parts can sound bare and sterile. In order to achieve the music's full effect the violinist is expected to follow the custom of the time and add improvised decorations and embellishments to the basic melodic line. (Some scholars even suggest that it is stylistically correct to use ornaments in the fast movements, as well as the slow.)

The unique **Violin and Harpsichord Sonata, Op. 5, No. 12,**

"La Folia," contains a set of twenty-three variations on an old Portuguese dance tune called "Folia." While originally a fast rhythmic dance performed by men dressed as women to the accompaniment of tambourine, the Folia melody had become sedate and stately by Corelli's time. In addition to Corelli, the same melody has intrigued a number of other composers, from such contemporaries as Bach and Vivaldi to Liszt and Rachmaninoff in more recent times, all of whom have used it as the basis for sets of variations.

The twelve sonatas that make up Op. 5, first published in 1700, were believed to have been composed over the previous three years. These sonatas became immensely popular immediately after publication, and many other editions appeared during Corelli's lifetime and after his death.

Claude Debussy

Born August 22, 1862, in Saint-Germain-en-Laye, France
Died March 25, 1918, in Paris

FOR most of his life, Claude Debussy tended to write music with specific titles—ranging from *Prélude à L'après-midi d'un faune* to *Nocturnes, Images,* and *La Mer.* The titles were less guides to programmatic content than references to the evocative qualities of the music—the sensations, feelings, atmosphere, and fleeting impressions that each composition called forth. In the final years of his life, though, Debussy changed his approach and gave his pieces names that had no specific connotations. Examples are his Études for piano and his three sonatas for different instrumental combinations—cello and piano; flute, viola, and harp; and violin and piano.

In part this inclination toward a more absolute, Classical approach sprang from his desire to return to the musical ideals of the great eighteenth-century French composers François Couperin (1668–1733) and Jean-Philippe Rameau (1683–1764). But while he was inclining toward a more Classical conception, Debussy was also rebelling against the idea of using predetermined formal structures. "I am more and more convinced," he wrote, "that music, by its very nature, is something that cannot be cast into a traditional and fixed form. It is made up of colors and rhythms. The rest is a lot of humbug invented by frigid imbeciles riding on the backs of the Masters." Moreover, he was extremely eager to rid himself of what he perceived to be the German domination of French music.

Two other factors also significantly influenced Debussy's final works: the discovery in 1909 that he had cancer and the August 1914 outbreak of World War I. The disease, which led to ever increasing pain, weakness, and general malaise, forced Debussy to endure much suffering over the final nine years of his life, while the outbreak of hostilities left him unable to compose or even go near the piano. "Never in any era," he observed, "have art and war been good bedfellows."

After composing virtually nothing during 1914, Debussy took up his pen again in the summer of 1915, completing first his Twelve Études. He then began work on what he planned to be Six Sonates pour Divers Instruments, of which he only lived to compose three. All were signed Claude Debussy, *Musicien Français,* firmly asserting the music's Gallic origins; all were dedicated to his wife, Emma Claude.

The **Sonata for Cello and Piano,** which Debussy wrote in July and August 1915, was first entitled "Pierrot fasche avec la lune," reflecting the composer's fascination with the Harlequin character, whose white mask and clown costume hid a soul filled with yearning and unfulfilled desire. On another level, Debussy seemed to be saying that his own disguise had been stripped away, forcing him to contemplate his terrible anguish and solitude.

The declamatory Prologue superimposes a nobility of character on an underlying pervasive melancholy. Of the work's organization, Debussy wrote, "The proportions and the form of the Sonata were almost classical in the true sense of the word." While the structure bears little resemblance to traditional sonata-allegro form, Debussy does allow the music to grow and develop organically from two melodic cells—one a rapid up-and-down turn (which is alluded to in the subsequent movements) and the other a slow, descending three-note figure. Speaking of this and the subsequent movements, Debussy wrote, "The piano must not fight the cello, but accompany it."

The following Serenade does indeed call to mind the hapless Harlequin serenading the indifferent Columbine, but with a somewhat sardonic air. Debussy calls on the cellist to use a number of technical tricks, from strumming pizzicato to producing high whistling harmonics, which succeed in bringing to mind such traditional serenade instruments as the guitar and flute.

The concluding Finale, which follows without pause, has elements of robust good humor and folklike vigor that had not been heard before in the sonata. Still, the impression persists that the high spirits are only superficial. Debussy interrupts the proceedings at one point for a brief, poignant interlude, marked *con morbidezza* (meaning "softly and gently," not "morbidly," as some interpreters believe), which exposes his deep anguish and feelings of isolation. As though embarrassed by this intimate confession, Debussy quickly assumes the clown guise once more and returns to the jolly cheerfulness of the movement's early section.

After the Cello Sonata, Debussy immediately turned to the Sonata for Flute, Viola, and Harp, which he composed during September and October of 1915. Soon afterward his health took a serious turn for the worse and he had to return from his vacation home, near Dieppe, to Paris. From Paris Debussy wrote to his friend the American violinist Arthur Hartmann that he was spiritually ready to write the violin sonata he had promised him, but that his deteriorating health made him wonder when he would be able to start composing. In December 1915, major surgery arrested the spread of Debussy's cancer, but it was followed by a debilitating course of radium treatments and chemotherapy, along with prescribed morphine to control the agonizing pain.

Finally, in the winter of 1916–1917, Debussy began work on the **Sonata for Violin and Piano,** completing it early that spring. Although the Violin Sonata proved to be the last composition of a terminally ill man, this animated, whimsical, and flamboyant work bears no air of the sickroom. Far from using the music to bid adieu, the composer adventuresomely sets out to explore new modes of expression.

Of the three final sonatas of his last years, this one best shows how Debussy adapts traditional sonata concepts to his uniquely personal expressive needs. The sonata starts with the violin presentation of a pair of musical gestures—the slow descent of two broken chords, followed by an up-and-down flutter of more rapid notes. After the statement and extension of these ideas, Debussy introduces a new section of considerable rhythmic ambiguity, in which the violin plays various figures over a lightly rippling background in the piano. Gradually a return of the opening ideas emerges, followed by a coda that builds up to some climactic moments.

In his book *Violin and Keyboard,* Abram Loft points out how the second movement, marked "Fantastique et léger," builds on a structural block of three descending chromatic notes. Heard at the outset in the piano, the idea is immediately taken up in the three long trilled notes of the violin, and appears in various guises and inversions throughout the movement. Although essentially sunny and droll in character, the movement reveals some strains of tender melancholy.

Commenting on the last movement of the Violin Sonata in a letter to his friend Robert Godet, Debussy wrote, "In the future beware of works that seem to have been planned under a clear blue sky; often they have stagnated in a dark, morose brain. Thus, the finale of this sonata goes through the most curious deformation to join in a game on a simple theme that turns back on itself, like a serpent biting its own tail." The theme he refers to occurs after a brief reminder of the first-movement motifs and is played by the unaccompanied violin. Organized into a rondolike form, with five transformations of the serpent-biting-its-tail theme appearing between contrasting interludes, the movement is a saucy, sensuous conclusion to the entire work.

Gabriel Fauré

Born May 12, 1845, in Pamiers, France
Died November 4, 1924, in Paris

ARDENT, elegant, refined, urbane, graceful—these are some of the adjectives that describe the music of Gabriel Fauré, judged by many to be the most outstanding musical figure to appear in France between Berlioz and Debussy. Confining himself almost exclusively to the smaller forms—songs, chamber works, piano pieces—Fauré left no symphonies or concertos; his two largest works are his Requiem and the opera *Pénélope*.

Although Fauré wrote four sonatas—two for violin and piano and two for cello and piano—only the first violin sonata was composed before he reached the age of seventy. Written when the composer was thirty, the **Sonata for Violin and Piano No. 1 in A, Op. 13**, is probably the most popular of all of his sonatas. Interestingly enough, no French publisher was interested in putting it out. Finally, on the intercession of a friend, the German firm Breitkopf & Härtel agreed to publish the work, but without any payment to the composer.

The piano states the first theme, with the melody notes embedded in the rapid figuration that continues almost without stop throughout the movement. The violin takes the theme up next and the two instruments easily pass the tune back and forth for the rest of this impassioned, lyrical movement. In fact, so much melodic interchange occurs that there are moments when the music sounds canonical, with one instrument imitating the other. Some commentators have even speculated that Fauré derived his inspiration from César Franck's better-known Violin Sonata, also in A major, oblivious of the fact that Franck wrote his sonata a decade later. As Charles Koechlin, one of Fauré's pupils, exclaimed, "Render unto Gabriel [Fauré], and not unto 'César,' that which is Gabriel's."

Although the highly expressive and deeply moving second movement, Andante, includes moments of deep pathos, the ending is suffused with a feeling of great calm and serene acceptance.

In contrast, the scherzo that follows fairly crackles with electricity. Basically scalar in thematic shape, Fauré provides one slower-moving interlude that is little more than a transformation of the first subject, before returning to the original character.

A strong, vigorous rhythmic impulse immediately establishes the character of the finale and continues, with but few instances of relaxation and some highly intense climaxes, right through to the end.

In the forty years that intervened between his first and second violin sonatas, much happened in Fauré's musical life. In 1896 he was appointed organist at the Madeleine and professor of composition at the Paris Conservatoire, becoming director there in 1905. In 1903, around the time he first became aware that he was growing deaf, Fauré became a music critic for *Le Figaro* (a fact noted with great glee by those who are convinced that an aural deficiency is a prerequisite for writing musical criticism!). By the time he composed his **Sonata for Violin and Piano No. 2 in E minor, Op. 108,** in 1916, at age seventy-one, he had completely lost his sense of hearing and was suffering from a chronic bronchial condition as well.

The opening movement of the second sonata sounds generally agitated and febrile, despite a subsidiary theme that introduces some quiet tenderness into the proceedings. The Andante, probably the most moving and most effective movement in the work, melds strength with repose. Fauré drew the theme from a symphony that he had written thirty-two years earlier but suppressed after one performance. Bright and cheerful, the Finale is informed by a youthful ardor and impetuosity that is hard to reconcile with the composer's advanced age.

Fauré composed his **Sonata for Cello and Piano No. 1 in D**

minor, **Op. 109,** in 1918 and his **Sonata for Cello and Piano
No. 2 in G minor, Op. 117,** three years later. Both came within
six years of his death in 1924 at age seventy-nine. The two pieces
bear several close resemblances: both demonstrate the composer's love for the cello's rich, opulent low range; both give the
piano a subsidiary role; and the three movements of both are
identically marked Allegro, Andante, Finale.

Op. 109 starts with a serious, somber movement that moves
forward in rhythmic fits and starts. A simple, rather melancholy
slow movement follows, leading to the vigorous Finale, with a
more important piano part than was heard earlier.

The Op. 117 opening strikes a more winsome, even joyous
note, in comparison with Op. 109. Fauré took the theme for the
Andante from a piece he had written earlier commemorating the
centenary of Napoleon's death; even though the music moves
languidly, the mood grows quite cheerful for the ending. The
sonata concludes with a Finale of almost riotous abandon, filled
with gleeful scales and arpeggios that provide a very positive,
upbeat culmination to the sonata.

César Franck

Born December 10, 1822 in Liège, Belgium
Died November 8, 1890, in Paris

BY all accounts, César Franck was an amazingly kind, gentle, good-hearted man, with a strong religious and mystical bent, who looked on composing as an act of faith. Many consider the **Violin Sonata in A,** his sole essay in the form, to be Franck's best work; it probably receives more performances than any of his other comparatively limited number of compositions. Players and audiences alike seem to enjoy the wide range of musical expression that Franck explores, from deeply pious contemplation to high-spirited exuberance.

The Violin Sonata is often cited as an example of cyclical form, a structural organization in which thematic material carries over from one movement to the others. In the words of composer Vincent D'Indy, Franck's sonata is "the first and the purest model of the cyclical treatment of themes in the form of an instrumental sonata."

Although there can be little question that the sonata conforms to the definition of cyclical form, the composer did not actually conceive of it in precisely that way. Rather Franck spoke of inventing themes related to the basic theme; he called these derived melodies "cousins." Thus, he did not set out so much to transform and recast the original melody in subsequent movements as he allowed his imagination to create themes that were organically related to the melody with which he began.

The first three notes the violin plays constitute the germ cell that informs the entire sonata—simply stated it consists of a note, a higher note, and a return to the original note. Each of the sonata's four movements starts with the same melodic inflection and in the course of the work it emerges in any number of different characters and contexts.

For the first movement, Franck extends the three-note musical gesture into a flowing, lyrical line that functions as the main subject. Other thematic material that is closely or remotely related to the basic motif follows. Although the movement builds to two impassioned climaxes, it presents an overall character of nobility and elegance.

The all-important motif presents itself at the start of the second movement, but is disguised this time in a torrent of agitated, turbulent passagework in the piano. Franck creates this form of the theme by linking together a succession of up-and-down turns, giving the sensation of a rising melodic line with the ups and downs moving above and beneath the overall ascent. Brilliant and virtuosic writing for both instruments makes the second movement the perfect foil to the poised calmness that came before.

The free and rhapsodic Recitative-Fantasia that follows starts off as completely improvisatory in character, with many references to material from the previous movements. The latter section becomes much more lyrical as Franck spins the melody out into wonderful cantabile phrases that further investigate the up-and-down musical motif.

The last movement features several appearances of a canon, in which the two instruments play the same melody, but starting at different times. The melody itself has a long, sustained line, but very clearly commences with a new version of the three-note cell heard at the very outset. Crafted with great warmth and charm, the movement presents fresh views of the germinal melody. At the end, the movement picks up speed and builds to a bombastic climax and a loud, forceful conclusion.

Franck composed the sonata early in the fall of 1886 as he was approaching his sixty-fourth birthday. He dedicated it to his friend, the Belgian violinist Eugène Ysaÿe, who gave the first performance in Brussels on December 16, 1886.

Edvard Grieg

Born June 15, 1843, in Bergen, Norway
Died September 4, 1907, in Bergen

DURING the latter years of the nineteenth century the struggle for freedom from foreign domination, both political and cultural, occupied the people of many European nations. Composers in these countries manifested their antipathy to outside influences by drawing on their own musical heritage—indigenous folksongs and dances and particular turns of melody and rhythm —for the inspiration and source of their own original concert works. Among the better-known composers who are associated with this so-called nationalistic movement are Smetana and Dvořák in what is now Czechoslovakia, Borodin, Mussorgsky, and Rimsky-Korsakov in Russia, Elgar in England, Albéniz and Granados in Spain, Gade in Denmark, and Edvard Grieg in Norway.

Nationalistic elements were not always dominant in Grieg's music, however. His early works reflect the very strict academic training in traditional music practices he received in his studies at the Leipzig Conservatory from 1858 to 1862. It wasn't until the mid-1860s that the composer discovered the treasures of Norwegian national music and for the next twenty highly productive years, this influence colored his music to a greater or lesser degree.

Grieg composed a total of seventy-five opus numbers, the vast bulk of which consisted of miniatures—short, small-scale piano pieces and songs—no more than a few minutes in length. Despite the fact that the creation of more extended works did not come easily to him, Grieg persevered. As he commented in 1877, "I will fight my way through the larger forms, cost what it may." A total of seven extensive works came out of this struggle —the well-known piano concerto, an unpublished symphony, and five sonatas. These sonatas, which span the central years of his life, from 1865 to 1887, show the effects of both the rise and the decline of Norwegian folk influence on his music.

Grieg composed his first two sonatas in June 1865 while on holiday in Rungsted, a resort on the coast of Denmark just north of Copenhagen. He described the period as "a happy time of joyful excitement and production." In an 1893 interview he reported, "Whether it was the enchanting surroundings or the stimulating air that inspired me, I cannot say. Enough that in eleven days I had composed my piano sonata and very soon after my first violin sonata."

The joyful **Piano Sonata, Op. 7,** brims over with youthful vigor, confidence, and the ability to make musical points in the most concise and economical way. The virtuosic first movement surges forward with great passion and energy, building to a climax at the very end. The Andante molto is antithetical in temperament—mostly quiet and simple with a tender pastoral quality, except for the more agitated middle section. The following minuet is also in three parts—the strong, stolid opening and closing sections framing a light, wistful center. The finale recaptures the vitality and tempestuous character of the first movement.

The **Sonata No. 1 for Violin and Piano, Op. 8,** enjoyed greater success than Grieg's other sonatas during his lifetime, and endures as a work of great charm and appeal. The opening movement is crammed full of delightful melodic motifs, each one vying with the next for the listener's attention. Grieg's Norwegian heritage comes to the fore in the second movement, with an opening section that derives from the indigenous *springdans,* a gay leaping folk dance. The contrasting middle part brings to mind the Hardanger fiddle, a Norwegian folk violin that includes a drone string, which gives the effect of a bagpipe. The use of short, repeated phrases contributes to the last movement's folklike character, but Grieg inserts a brief fugato, a sort of nod of acknowledgment to his academic training in Leipzig.

Even more indebted to Norwegian national music is the So-nata No. 2 for Violin and Piano, Op. 13, which Grieg composed in three weeks in July 1867, while he was living in Christiania (now Oslo). The work comes across as glowing and buoyant, permeated with joyful folk elements. Despite the many melodies and rhythms of folk character heard here and elsewhere, all originated with Grieg and have never been traced to any other source.

Following the slow and pensive opening of the sonata's first movement, the music breaks into the happy steps of a springdans for the balance of the first movement. Although the tempo designation of the second movement is Allegretto tranquillo alla Romanza ("Rather fast; calm and songlike"), folk-dance rhythms erupt from time to time and the movement ends with a good imitation of a country fiddler's sounds. The finale, like the opening movement, evokes the exuberance of a vigorous peasant dance.

Some years later, Grieg reported what happened right after the premiere of the Op. 13 Violin Sonata. "Gade [a prominent Danish composer] came to the artist's room and said, 'No, Grieg, you must not make the next sonata as Norwegian.' I had at that moment tasted blood and answered, 'Yes, Professor, the next one is going to be even worse.' "

In spite of Grieg's threat, the work that followed, the Sonata for Cello and Piano, Op. 36, was not very different from his earlier sonatas. Composed in Bergen in the spring of 1883, the piece was dedicated to Grieg's older brother, John, an amateur cellist. It proved to be a difficult piece to compose. "To all appearances," Grieg wrote in December 1882, "I am living a more peaceful life than ever before, but in reality it is a life full of inward struggle. I am both spiritually and bodily unwell and decide every other day not to compose another note, because I satisfy myself less and less."

In some ways the sonata lacks some of the excitement and enthusiasm of his earlier works. But the first movement is a paradigm of writing for the cello, exploiting fully the unique qualities of that instrument's rich, sonorous tone and including a brief cadenza. The main theme of the slow movement sounds very much like the noble Triumphal March from Grieg's incidental music to *Sigurd Jorsalfar.* And the slow, mysterious introduction for cello alone that opens the last movement soon plunges into a wild, spirited dance related to the Norwegian *halling,* an acrobatic folk dance that includes high kicks and somersaults.

Grieg completed his final and probably most frequently performed sonata, the **Sonata No. 3 for Violin and Piano, Op. 45,** in January 1887. The immediate inspiration for the sonata was a visit the twenty-year-old Italian violinist Teresina Tua paid Grieg in the fall of 1886. Grieg called Signorina Tua "the little fiddlefairy on my troll-hill," and said it was for her that he would "again . . . perpetrate something for the violin." But Grieg was also much influenced by the Franck Violin Sonata and the Brahms Op. 100 Violin Sonata, both of which he heard that year. Impressed by their style and compositional approach, Grieg wrote a sonata that was more cosmopolitan and drew less on Norwegian sources than the others. (In tracing the evolution of his three violin sonatas Grieg later said, "They represent periods in my development—the first naive, rich in ideas; the second national; and the third with a wider horizon.")

The tragic sweep of the first movement contains a dark, threatening first theme and a more tranquil second theme that eventually triumphs over the angry mood of the opening. The character lightens for the middle movement, which sparkles with light and surges with nobility of feeling. But the happiness does not long endure. The last movement emerges predominantly tragic despite an ending that soars with a grandiose version of the subsidiary theme.

George Frideric Handel

Born February 23, 1685, in Halle, Germany
Died April 14, 1759, in London

THE public associates the name Handel mainly with one piece of music—*Messiah.* Few are aware of the composer's vast output, which includes some fifty operas (several of which are in the current repertoires of opera houses around the world), more than twenty oratorios besides *Messiah* (such as *Israel in Egypt* and *Judas Maccabeus),* and a considerable number of vocal and instrumental pieces, comprising eighteen concerti grossi, sixteen organ concertos, numerous suites and miscellaneous compositions, sixteen trio sonatas, and fifteen duo sonatas.

Handel probably composed his duo sonatas while Kapellmeister to the Elector of Hanover in Germany from 1710 to 1712. The works were first published in 1722 under the title **15 Sonatas for Flute, Oboe or Violin with Thoroughbass for Harpsichord or Bass Viol, Op. 1.** Within this one opus there are seven sonatas for flute (Numbers 1, 2, 4, 5, 7, 9, and 11), two sonatas for oboe (Numbers 6 and 8), and six sonatas for violin (Numbers 3, 10, 12, 13, 14, and 15).

The thoroughbass referred to in the title and also known as figured bass or *basso continuo,* is an eighteenth-century style of harpsichord writing that includes just a single line of left-hand bass notes. Numbers and symbols under the notes indicate the exact harmonies the harpsichordist should build on the bass line, but leave the exact distribution of the notes to the player's discretion.

Although Handel originally conceived these sonatas to be performed by three players—the melody line by flute, oboe, or violin, with harpsichord and cello or bass viol handling the thoroughbass, today's presentations almost always involve only two players—the melody instrument and the keyboard instrument alone. In some concerts the keyboard performer plays the part on a piano, which is generally more readily available than a harpsichord. And while the first publication showed only the bass line, most modern editions include a full harpsichord part, with the thoroughbass worked out, or "realized," and printed in the music.

Of the fifteen sonatas, ten contain four movements; three have five movements; one has three movements; and one has seven. The four-movement sonatas always follow the same order of Slow, Fast, Slow, Fast tempos. In general, the first movement is substantial in length, serious, and makes frequent use of dotted (long-short) rhythms. High energy and great vigor usually identify the second movement; a good number also contain passages of imitative counterpoint. Quite often the third movement—slow tempo, songlike character, and short length—functions as little more than an introduction to the last movement. Although not directed to do so in the score, many performers go directly from the third to the fourth movement with little or no break. The finale, the brightest and lightest movement of the sonata, is commonly in a sprightly dancelike rhythm.

Franz Joseph Haydn

Born March 31, 1732, in Rohrau, Austria
Died May 31, 1809, in Vienna

A GENIUS is sometimes defined as the right person in the right place at the right time. If so, Haydn most assuredly qualifies for the appellation. When he started composing in the late 1750s, music was entering a period of rapid and considerable change, with Vienna at the epicenter of the upheaval. Imbued with the vision to synthesize the emerging elements of the musical revolution with the enduring contributions from the past, Haydn forged a new style that served as the foundation for the continued development and transformation of music.

Among the major tendencies that Haydn was able to integrate were the following: the somewhat anachronistic Baroque style, with its dependence on counterpoint and the maintenance of a single character or "affection" in each individual movement or piece; the Rococo and *style galant,* which placed a premium on lightness of touch, charm, and elegance and began to replace the Baroque around 1740; and the subsequent *Sturm und Drang* spirit, which introduced a new and heightened emotional intensity, urgency, and energy into music. In addition, Haydn had the ability to see the potential in the inchoate sonata-allegro form, and to raise it to the highest level of musical expressivity. He also developed both the standard instrumentation of such performing groups as the symphony orchestra, string quartet, and piano trio, and the most effective style of composing for such organizations.

To the foregoing factors Haydn added the so-called learned

style, a complex, intellectually challenging texture and structure. On a more personal level, he invented themes that harked back to the peasant melodies and rhythms recalled from his youth. And above all, he sought innovative means of expression and novel techniques with a zeal and enthusiasm that contradicted his stereotypical representation as the bewigged paterfamilias.

Although better known for his symphonies, oratorios, and chamber music, Haydn also wrote a total of sixty-two piano sonatas, starting just before 1760 and completing the last one in 1794. Through them one can trace the composer's growing skill and mastery, as well as his increasing success in combining the roiling currents of eighteenth-century musical practice.

While scholars have been successful in placing Haydn's symphonies and chamber music into chronological order, they have had much more difficulty with his piano sonatas. The first reasonably accurate catalog, prepared by Karl Pasler just after World War I, contained only fifty-two sonatas. More recently, Anthony van Hoboken's 1957 thematic catalog, based on Pasler's work, assigned a Hoboken number to each of the sonatas and became the widely accepted standard. Finally, in 1964 Christa Landon's *Wiener Urtext Ausgabe* expanded the list to sixty-two sonatas and corrected the Hoboken catalog; the WUA number is used here, with the Hoboken number following in parentheses.

Haydn's sonatas can be divided into three periods. The first covers the initial twenty-eight sonatas (18 in Hoboken) and extends from the late 1750s until about 1766. Even though most are called sonatas (a few are called partitas), they all model their form more on the divertimento or suite. Rococo in character, the pieces are small, short, and light toned— essentially sets of brief, dancelike pieces in the same key. Generally speaking, each contains a minuet as either the second or third movement. While intended for the piano, the writing inclines toward the harpsichord style. Of these early works, perhaps the best known is the **Piano Sonata in G, WUA 5 (XVI: 11)**, a delightful miniature, only four pages long, with a third-movement minuet.

Sonatas WUA 29 to 57 (XVI: 19 to 47) constitute the second group; they were composed between 1766 and 1788, a time when Haydn was musically isolated, spending most of each year as Kapellmeister at the Esterházy palace, located far from any large city or musical center. During this period Haydn experimented with new styles and techniques, creating works that are more serious, expressive, dramatic, and profound than those that came before. Two of these sonatas—the **Piano Sonata in E flat, WUA 29 (XVI: 45)**, and **Piano Sonata in A flat, WUA 31 (XVI: 46)**—are first-rate creations, big in scope and showing a firm grasp of technique. Among the more outstanding is **Piano Sonata in C minor, WUA 33 (XVI: 20)**, a romantic masterpiece of great tragic power that approaches symphonic proportions and furnishes an outstanding example of *Sturm und Drang*. The outside movements are especially striking; the first overflows with intense passion, while the third provides an angry, dramatic climax to the entire sonata.

The last five sonatas, WUA 58 to 62 (XVI: 48 to 52), composed from 1790 to 1794, conclude nearly a half century of writing for the piano. These works find Haydn at the very height of his powers, perfectly integrating into a satisfying whole the various elements that had been running through his music over the many decades.

The **Piano Sonata in C, WUA 58 (XVI: 48)**, consists of two movements. The first comprises a set of variations, alternately in major and minor, on a beautifully lyrical theme; the second is a brilliant rondo.

The **Piano Sonata in E flat, WUA 59 (XVI: 49)**, which held special meaning for the composer, was dedicated to Marianne von Genzinger, wife of Prince Nicholas Esterházy's physician and Haydn's very dear friend. In a letter to Marianne, Haydn informed the dedicatee that the Adagio "has a deep significance that I will analyze for you when the opportunity arises." While Haydn may have discussed the specific meaning with Madame von Genzinger, the allusion has eluded scholars. The opening movement of this rather small-scale work sounds basically monothematic; the second theme clearly grows out of the first. The second movement is the one with "deep significance," while the third conveys a sense of gaiety and cheerfulness.

While on an extended visit to London in 1794, Haydn composed the last three sonatas, which reached a level of even greater expressivity and mastery than he had achieved heretofore. Dedicated to Theresa Jansen (later Mrs. Bartolozzi), the **Piano Sonata in C, WUA 60 (XVI: 50)**, opens magically as single, isolated notes gain speed and momentum and quickly build to a wonderfully satisfying climax. The second theme, as so often occurs in Haydn, is essentially a variant of the first. The lovely slow movement, a reworking of an earlier Adagio, bears a somewhat impersonal air. And the jocular finale rushes along with lighthearted whimsy and humorous banter.

Haydn as experimenter comes to the fore in the two-movement **Piano Sonata in D, WUA 61 (XVI: 51)**. The quite slow first movement offers a very free realization of the standard structural elements in sonata-allegro form. The principal theme, a lyrical melody, very romantic in character, could have been written by Schubert. The fast and fiery second movement is organized in a two-part form that bears only the most distant relationship to sonata-allegro.

The final **Piano Sonata in E flat, WUA 62 (XVI: 52)**, belongs in the small group of true masterworks, a position earned by virtue of its bold harmonies, inspired lyricism, confident technique, and the stunning virtuosity of its piano writing. The first movement has a heroic, monumental character that is somewhat lightened by the subsidiary theme, a melody very obviously derived from the opening. Cast in a remote key (E major, after E-flat major), the Adagio starts with a rhythmic pattern that continues throughout; this profound movement ranks high among Haydn's inspirations. The finale provides a happy cap to the proceedings, glinting with touches of humor and making exceptionally good use of pauses and silences.

Paul Hindemith

Born November 16, 1895, in Hanau, Germany
Died December 28, 1963, in Frankfurt

ABOVE the score of his Sonata for Alto Horn and Piano, Hindemith inscribed a short original poem for the players to read aloud before playing the last movement. The final three lines of the poem are perhaps the most succinct summary of Hindemith's approach to music:

> Your task it is, amid confusion, rush, and noise
> To grasp the lasting, calm, and meaningful,
> And finding it anew, to hold and treasure it.

In musical terms, Hindemith's accepted goal was to adapt traditional compositional practices to his twentieth-century expressive needs. The result was a style that is usually referred to as Neoclassicism—music that is direct and clear in form, contrapuntal in texture, and restrained in expression. But acting as a counterbalance to this fundamental tendency was Hindemith's keen sensitivity to the world in which he lived and the strong impact of contemporary political, social, and cultural events and beliefs on his creativity.

Hindemith's earliest compositions show elements of Dadaism —the use of unexpected, absurd, and seemingly nonsensical musical devices to jar, shock, and discomfort listeners, and Expressionism—the impassioned use of melodies, rhythms, and harmonies to give vivid expression to the artist's innermost feelings and emotions. Around 1923, Hindemith completely rejected Expressionism and embraced the aesthetic credo of *Neue Sach-*

lichkeit ("New Objectivity"), striving for intense, energized, linear construction, great clarity, and tight, highly logical control, with a good measure of strength verging on the brutal.

Several years later Hindemith began to effect a synthesis between *Neue Sachlichkeit* and *Jugendmusik*—a movement that promoted music making by young people and amateurs as a way of obliterating the barriers between composers, performers, and the public. This style came to be known as *Gebrauchsmusik,* "music for use" or "utility music." Hindemith summed up the artistic philosophy of *Gebrauchsmusik* by saying, "A composer should write today only if he knows for what purpose he is writing. The days of composing for the sake of composing are perhaps gone forever."

Surely one of the most naturally gifted and innately talented musicians of this century, Hindemith was, in Alfred Einstein's words, "simply a musician who produces music as a tree bears fruit," a view seconded by Paul Bekker, who commented, "He doesn't compose, he musics."

Soon after completing his first sonata, the **Sonata for Violin and Piano, Op. 11, No. 1,** in 1918, Hindemith wrote, "I want to compose a whole series of sonatas. Each of them is to be completely different from the preceding ones. I want to see whether I can't, in a whole series of such pieces, increase the potentialities (which are not very great in this type of music and this combination) and extend the horizon."

Hindemith's statement, which referred primarily to violin and piano sonatas, came to include all the works he wrote in this form. Although his first sonatas, composed from 1918 through 1924, were exclusively for string instruments—violin, viola, and cello, with one for viola d'amore—starting in 1935 he ventured far afield, writing for virtually every instrument. By the time he reached his last sonata, the **Sonata for Tuba and Piano,** in 1955, Hindemith had created a total of forty sonatas, four of which remain unpublished.

PUBLISHED SONATAS

1918   Violin and Piano, Op. 11, No. 1
       Violin and Piano, Op. 11, No. 2

1919   Viola and Piano, Op. 11, No. 4
       Solo Viola, Op. 11, No. 5
       Cello and Piano, Op. 11, No. 3

1922   Solo Viola, Op. 25, No. 1
       Viola d'Amore and Piano, Op. 25, No. 2
       Solo Cello, Op. 25, No. 3
       Viola and Piano, Op. 25, No. 4

1924   Solo Violin, Op. 31, No. 1
       Solo Violin, Op. 31, No. 2

1935   Violin and Piano*

1936   Three for Piano
       Flute and Piano

1937   Two for Organ

1938   Bassoon and Piano
       Oboe and Piano
       Piano, four hands

1939   Viola and Piano
       Violin and Piano
       Clarinet and Piano
       Harp
       Horn and Piano
       Trumpet and Piano

1940   Organ

1941   English Horn and Piano
       Trombone and Piano

1942   Two Pianos

1943   Alto Horn and Piano

1948   Cello and Piano

1949   Double Bass and Piano

1952   Four Horns and Piano

1955   Tuba and Piano

Almost all of the sonatas are abstract, lacking any programmatic or symbolic significance. Only three have references out-

* (From now on, Hindemith no longer used opus numbers.)

side the music: **Sonata for Alto Horn and Piano** includes Hindemith's poem "The Posthorn," which is to be read out loud by the two performers before playing the final movement. It begins:

> Is not the sounding of a horn to our busy soul
> Like a sonorous visit from those ages
> Which counted speed by straining horses' gallop,
> And not by lightning prisoned up in cable;

It ends with the quotation given on page 110. **Piano Sonata No. 1** was inspired by Friedrich Hölderlin's poem "Der Main." And the *Rezitativ* movement of **Sonata for Two Pianos** suggests a perfect, but unsung, setting of the medieval English poem "This World's Joy."

Four of Hindemith's sonatas for viola, the instrument on which he excelled as a performer, are of special interest. Two sonatas reflect the composer's fascination with Debussy, the **Sonata for Viola and Piano, Op. 11, No. 4,** and **Sonata for Solo Viola, Op. 11, No. 5;** the others—the **Sonata for Solo Viola, Op. 25, No. 1,** and **Sonata for Viola and Piano, Op. 25, no. 4** —are often cited as paradigms of *Neue Sachlichkeit* in music.

Each of the sonatas can be said to be idiomatically written for the particular instrument. This is easily understood when one realizes that Hindemith played the viola, violin, and viola d'amore on a professional level and was a competent player on more than a dozen other instruments.

Even though Hindemith composed his sonatas in a variety of styles, one can sense a gradual evolutionary change, moving from the experimentation of his early sonatas toward a greater acceptance of Neoclassicism in his later essays.

Charles Ives

Born October 20, 1874, in Danbury, Connecticut
Died May 19, 1954, in New York City

CHARLES IVES consistently earns high praise as America's foremost experimental and iconoclastic composer. A good number of commentators have even gone so far as to single Ives out as the greatest composer this country has ever produced.

Many factors gave shape and style to Ives's music. A major consideration was his father, George, who was the bandmaster and leading music teacher in Danbury. George Ives stirred his son's imagination with fanciful and innovative efforts to capture in music everything from the sound of a sneeze, to a church congregation singing out of tune, to the mingled sounds of two bands playing different marches in a parade. Also significant were Ives's years as a student at Yale University, where he received strict academic training in traditional music practices and learned to impose order and technique on the untrammeled urge to seek the new and novel that he got from his father.

To these early influences must be added Ives's belief in transcendentalism—a search for reality through spiritual intuition. Central to this philosophy is the belief that even the most ordinary things possess an essential spirit and that this spirit pervades the entire universe, creating a unity of all existence. Ralph Waldo Emerson, one of the leading lights of transcendentalism, stated, "All things are one." In Ives's words, "The fabric of existence weaves itself whole." This philosophy was so basic to Ives's being that it allowed him to combine such seemingly disparate musical elements as hymn tunes, popular songs, country-fiddle dances, and Beethoven symphonies in his original compositions.

And finally, though Ives was familiar with all the standard musical forms, he preferred to follow his own stream of musical consciousness, allowing the music to find its own design, rather than trying to fit it into a predetermined formal structure. Because he was an immensely successful businessman he never felt it necessary to tailor his style to please performers or audiences, despite his desperate desire to have his music performed.

Ives wrote seven sonatas—two for piano and five for violin. (There is also a short piano piece, *Three-Page Sonata*, of 1905.)

Piano Sonatas

The mammoth **Piano Sonata No. 1,** in five movements, takes more than a half hour to perform. The composer once described it as "a kind of impression, remembrance, and reflection of the country life in some of the Connecticut villages in the 1880s and 1890s." More specifically, Ives gave this movement-by-movement program: "The family together in the first and last movements, the boy sowing oats in the ragtimes [movements two and four], and the parental anxiety in the middle movement."

Quotations from outside sources pervade the entire sonata, ranging from gospel songs (such as "I Was a Wandering Sheep" and "What a Friend We Have in Jesus") to popular songs of the day (such as "Oh, Susannah" and "How Dry I Am"). Quite apparent, too, is a distinctive three-note descending motif that occurs any number of times in each movement. Although Ives completed the sonata in 1910, it was not until 1949 that the work received its premiere, played in New York City by William Masselos.

Many consider the **Piano Sonata No. 2, "Concord, Mass., 1840–1860"** to be Ives's finest work. The composer describes it as "a group of four pieces called sonata for want of a more exact name. The whole is an attempt to present one person's impression of the spirit of transcendentalism that is associated in the minds of many with Concord, Massachusetts, of over a half century ago."

Each of the four movements takes its name from an important literary figure. The first carries the title "Emerson," whom Ives describes as "explorer of the spiritual immensities," saying that the music is made up "of contrasts—dramatic, lyrical, barbed, restrained, tone clusters, silences." Ives asks a violist to join the pianist and play the special melody that occurs near the end of this powerful movement.

"Hawthorne," a scherzo, expresses some of this American writer's "wilder, fantastical adventures in the half-childlike, half-fairylike phantastical realms." At one point in this energetic movement, with its ragtime rhythms, Ives directs the player to hold a wooden board—exactly 14¾ inches long—down on the keys, so those notes will ring out, their strings set into vibration by the overtones of the bass notes that are being played.

"The Alcotts" section attempts "to catch something of that common sentiment . . . a strength of hope that never gives way to despair, a conviction in the power of the common soul." This lyrical slow movement, perhaps the most accessible of the sonata, communicates very directly through wonderfully simple means.

"Thoreau," a quiet, introspective movement, depicts a day spent meditating and communing with nature at Walden Pond. Near the end Ives inserts a short melody for flute, explaining, "Thoreau much prefers to hear the flute over Walden."

Completed in 1915, Ives published the "Concord" Sonata at his own expense in 1919, but had to wait twenty years for its premiere, which was given by John Kirkpatrick in New York City.

Violin Sonatas

Ives finished all five of his violin sonatas within a few years—between 1908 and 1916, approximately. Although he was to live nearly forty years longer, Ives almost completely stopped composing soon after his last violin sonata. Among the explanations are the pressures of his business, a severe heart attack and chronic diabetes that left him severely disabled, his distress at the entry of the United States into World War I, and his profound disappointment over the public's lack of interest in his music.

Like so many of his other compositions, the five violin sonatas contain excerpts from church hymns as well as popular songs and dances; violinist Abram Loft counted nineteen quotations, ranging from "Jesus Loves Me" to "Turkey in the Straw." In his **Violin and Piano Sonata No. 1,** Ives actually wrote the words of the hymn "Watchman, Tell Us of the Night" under the melody, presumably to let the player know where to place the stresses and accents.

The three movements of the **Violin and Piano Sonata No. 2** have programmatic titles. The first, "Autumn," makes reference to the special beauties of that season in New England. "In the Barn," the second, seems closely modeled on a wild Saturday night barn dance. And the third, "The Revival," evokes the fervid singing at a camp-meeting revival service of the sort that Ives knew so well from his youth.

The composer sometimes referred to his **Violin and Piano Sonata No. 3** as a "weak sister." He claimed that, because of the harshness of the criticism his compositions were receiving, he found himself compromising his ideals, particularly in the third and fourth violin sonatas. No one, of course, knows exactly what form this compromise took; one can, however, point out the elements in the last movement that bring to mind the César Franck Violin Sonata.

For his **Violin and Piano Sonata No. 4,** subtitled "Children's Day at the Camp Meeting," Ives included the following notes:

The subject matter is . . . the children's services at the outdoor Summer camp meetings. The children made the most of it. They would at times get stirred up, excited and even boisterous, but underneath there was usually something serious.

The First Movement was suggested by an actual happening at one of these services. The children, especially the boys, liked to get up and join in the marching kind of hymns. And as these meetings were "out-door," the "march" sometimes became a real one.

The Second Movement is quieter and more serious. Most of the Movement moves around a rather quiet but old favorite Hymn of the children. But as usual, even in the quiet services, some of the deacon-enthusiasts would get up and sing, roar, pray and shout, but always fervently, seriously, reverently—perhaps not "artistically"—(perhaps the better for it).

The Third Movement is more of the nature of the First. As the boys get marching again some of the old men would join in and march as fast (sometimes) as the boys and sing what they felt.

There is also a Violin and Piano Sonata No. 5 which was unearthed recently by John Kirkpatrick and others and apparently was actually the third of the sonatas to be completed.

Zoltán Kodály

Born December 16, 1882, in Kecskemét, Hungary
Died March 6, 1967, in Budapest

AROUND 1905, while still a university student, Kodály became interested in the folk music of his native Hungary. After spending years collecting, studying, transcribing, and editing this music, he wrote his doctoral thesis, *Strophic Structure in the Hungarian Folk Song.* So intense was his involvement with Hungarian music that its melodies and rhythms became fully integrated into his musical vocabulary. He did not consciously set out to model his music on existent folksongs; his writing instinctively took on the inflections and turns of phrase of Hungarian national music.

In December 1909, while still very much under the folk music influence, Kodály began composing his **Sonata for Cello and Piano, Op. 4,** completing it in February of the following year. Although the first movement, Fantasia, exhibits some Impressionistic elements, it is much more closely identified with the Hungarian *czárdás,* a folk dance that always starts with a mournful, improvisatory-sounding lament called a *lassú.* A naive, repetitive theme, much like the gay tune of a children's folk dance or counting song, opens the second and final movement. Kodály introduces a slightly more somber theme, but the mood is mostly bright and spirited as he works through the two themes and ends the movement by making reference to the opening Fantasia.

The folk influence manifests itself somewhat more subtly in the **Sonata for Cello Solo, Op. 8,** of 1915. Most striking is the brilliant writing for the cello—taking the performer from the bottom to the very top of the cello register, including passages of incredible technical difficulty and eliciting amazing sounds and sonorities. Kodály asks that the performer change the tuning of the bottom two strings (called *scordatura*)—lowering the C and G strings to the notes B and F-sharp, thereby slightly extending the range and making it possible to play some figures that would otherwise be impossible. Along with the intricacy and speed of some of the passagework, Kodály presents the cello with many opportunities to sing out in full-voiced splendor. The three movements are, respectively, dramatic and intense, expansive with soaring cantilena melodies, and dazzling in technical display.

Franz Liszt

Born October 22, 1811, in Raiding, Hungary
Died July 31, 1886, in Bayreuth, Germany

LISZT was an extremely prolific composer—particularly for the
piano, with some 1,300 individual works to his credit—and pre-
eminent in his time as a pianist ("Bach is the foundation of piano
playing, Liszt is the summit," Ferruccio Busoni once observed).
Nevertheless, Liszt is credited with only one true piano sonata,
along with one questionable sonata for that instrument. Actually
Liszt composed eight sonatas, but five of them—three for solo
piano, one for piano duet, and one for violin and piano—are
juvenile works, and just a fragment remains of another piano
sonata.

Many consider Liszt's "Dante" Sonata questionable largely
because it departs so sharply from traditional sonata form and is
a programmatic, rather than an abstract, piece of music. Liszt
wrote it as the last work in the second set, the Italian set, of
piano pieces he called *Années de pèlerinage,* giving it the special
title *Une Fantaisie quasi Sonata après une lecture de Dante* ("A Fantasy, Somewhat like a Sonata, After a Reading of Dante"). For
many years, the Dante reference was widely believed to have
been inspired by Victor Hugo's poem on the subject. In point of
fact, Hugo's poem was published on August 6, 1837, and Liszt
completed the work in October 1837 (revising it in 1849), making it highly unlikely that the composer saw the poem while
writing the music. Even though the poetic reference was probably added later, the music, nonetheless, stunningly evokes the
Inferno and Paradise as described in Dante's *Divine Comedy.*

The sonata opens with a slow, portentous descending line that comes to a complete stop, clearly suggesting a musical analogue to Dante's words "Abandon hope all ye who enter here." The following section, which Liszt asked to be played *lamentoso,* projects a nervous agitated character while still maintaining the same downward motion. After building to a raging climax Liszt presents a choralelike theme whose slow, solemn tones are enveloped in plunging octave runs before being transformed into a lyrical love song. All the elements are combined and worked through in what can be considered a description of the Inferno. In the final section the chorale theme is put in a glowing, ethereal setting, evoking the beauties of Paradise. In the opinion of many commentators, however, hell is much more interesting than heaven—at least musically speaking.

Liszt's **B minor Piano Sonata,** which has no comparable extramusical associations, was written in 1852–1853, and proved to be the composer's last major work for piano. Some five years earlier he had withdrawn from his immensely successful career as a virtuoso pianist (nineteenth-century "groupies" collected locks of his long, flowing hair as avidly as rock and roll enthusiasts collect autographs and photos today), and after completing the sonata he wrote, "I shall have done for the present with the piano in order to devote myself exclusively to orchestral compositions."

In the B minor Sonata Liszt sought to break the bonds of traditional, Classical sonata form. He attempted to create a new approach to musical organization, one that combined flexibility and variety with an overall, binding unity. To accomplish his objective, Liszt wrote a continuous, thirty-minute, one-movement work in which each of the four interconnected sections serves a double function. That is, each section corresponds to the part of a single sonata-allegro movement, but also has the formal structure of an individual movement within a four-movement sonata, as shown below:

PART OF LISZT SONATA	FUNCTION IN SONATA-ALLEGRO FORM	INTERNAL FORM
SECTION 1 *Allegro energico*	exposition	sonatina form
SECTION 2 *Andante sostenuto*	development	three-part song form (ABA)
SECTION 3 *Fugato*	development continued	scherzo (ABA)
SECTION 4 *Finale*	recapitulation	sonatina form

Liszt presents several motifs in the short, slow introduction and the fast Allegro energico that follows; others come in later—principally a grandiose, expansive melody and a tender, lovely slow theme. He then creates the entire fabric of the sonata through a method known as *thematic transformation,* or metamorphosis, in which he interweaves these motifs—but always in different guises and shapes and almost never following the usual techniques of thematic development. Instead, Liszt transforms and recasts the individual motifs—the amorous becomes bellicose, the playful becomes foreboding, the angry becomes accepting, the frightening becomes ingenuous, the gloomy becomes bright, and so on. Thus, by working these changes on the comparatively limited melodic material, Liszt manages to fashion a work of unflagging interest and variety.

Most pianists find the B minor a fiendishly difficult work to play, requiring not only full mastery of all the very considerable technical problems, but the ability to rise above these concerns to make an important musical statement. At the same time, for full enjoyment and understanding, the listener must listen intently to hear the original statements of each melody and to catch them in their various incarnations throughout the piece.

Although Robert Schumann, to whom the sonata is dedicated, thought it an inferior piece and was terribly embarrassed to have his name associated with the work, and Brahms reportedly fell asleep when Liszt first played it for him, most people—performers and listeners alike—agree with the evaluation of the piece that Richard Wagner expressed to the composer: "The sonata is beautiful beyond all belief; huge, lovable, profound and exalted; stately as yourself."

Felix Mendelssohn

Born February 3, 1809, in Hamburg
Died November 4, 1847, in Leipzig

SURELY no other composer was as supremely favored as Mendelssohn. He was born into a highly cultured, immensely wealthy family that contributed in every possible way to his growth and development; he was an amazing musical prodigy, appearing in concerts and having his original compositions performed in public at age nine; as a mature composer, conductor, and performer he was held in the very highest esteem by his peers and the public alike; and he was well endowed with intelligence, education, and talent not only as a musician, but as a writer and artist as well.

Over the course of his short, thirty-eight-year life, Mendelssohn composed ten sonatas that he allowed to be published during his lifetime—six for organ, two for piano and cello, and one each for piano and for piano and violin. In the discussion below we also consider the two posthumously published piano sonatas. Of these dozen sonatas, four (three for piano and one for violin) were composed when Mendelssohn was between twelve and eighteen years old; the other eight (two for cello and six for organ) were written over a period of seven years, starting at age twenty-nine.

Composed in 1821, when Mendelssohn was only twelve years old, his **Piano Sonata in G minor, Op. 105,** was published in 1868 after the composer's death, and given this deceptively high opus number. Even though it is the earliest printed sonata, it already shows the composer in full possession of a solid compositional technique and exhibits great fluency of thematic invention. Overall, this is an imaginative, well-constructed sonata, even though it reveals the composer somewhat under the influence of Haydn's piano-writing style.

Four years later, in 1825, Mendelssohn wrote the **Sonata for Piano and Violin in F minor, Op. 4,** dedicating it to his good friend, violinist Eduard Rietz. While the work sounds somewhat derivative, using Mozart and Beethoven as stylistic models, it is distinguished by highly original harmonies and Romantic coloristic effects. The opening of the sonata attracts immediate attention with a passage for violin solo in which the instrument plays with great rhythmic freedom and fluidity. The rest of the movement ranges from sections of great drive and passion to parts that are much more poetic and sensitive. At first, the Poco adagio resembles a slow, sedate minuet, but it gradually grows more rhapsodic. The peak of the finale, a cadenzalike passage for the violin, leads to a quiet, dainty ending.

The **Piano Sonata in E, Op. 6,** the only piano sonata that Mendelssohn submitted for publication, was composed in 1826. While it clearly shows the influence of the Beethoven piano sonatas, strangely enough it does not contain one movement in standard sonata-allegro form. Made up of four movements played without pause, the first features lovely, lyrical, vocal-sounding themes that are fancifully treated with great ease and spontaneity. The delightful second movement seems like a minuet, but with some of the light qualities of a scherzo. The *Andante,* the high point of the sonata, has a rather sectional construction and at one point recalls the theme of the first movement. Perhaps somewhat overstated, the finale nevertheless captivates with its infectious gusto and vigor.

Bearing a strangely high opus number because of its posthumous publication, the **Piano Sonata in B flat, Op. 106,** dates from 1827 and counts as the last of Mendelssohn's teenage sonatas. Even more than the E major, the B-flat sonata shows the impact of Beethoven, particularly in the first movement, where the first theme resembles the opening of the older master's "Hammerklavier" Sonata and the second recalls his *Coriolan Overture.* The second movement successfully captures the scherzo spirit, but many pianists find the writing difficult and awkward to execute. Mendelssohn seems to have drawn the inspiration for the Andante from the barcarolle, the traditional Venetian boat song. A very dramatic interlude acts as a bridge to the finale, which is an amiable, ambling sort of rondo.

"This sonata is the purest kind of music, completely valid in and for itself—a sonata as beautiful and lucid as anything that has ever emerged from the hands of a great artist." Thus Robert Schumann described Mendelssohn's **Sonata for Piano and Cello No. 1 in B flat, Op. 45.** Completed in 1838 when the composer was twenty-nine years old and dedicated to his cellist brother Paul, the sonata is a pleasant, affable affair that moves effortlessly between warm and graceful sections and passages exhibiting more fire and drama. Of the three movements, the second stands out for its lovely autumnal, melancholy quality, epitomized by the gentle, sigh-like descending figure of the principal motif.

In comparison with the B-flat sonata, the **Sonata for Piano and Cello No. 2 in D, Op. 58,** of 1843 was written on a grander scale, and in the opinion of many, is the superior composition. The first movement opens with a bold, upward-reaching theme that also serves as the source of the subsidiary subject. Although highly energetic overall, the movement contains some moments of great reflective beauty. Conceived with wonderful wit and humor, the scherzo second movement abounds with appeal and charm; of special interest is the middle section in which the cello alternately plays with the bow *(arco)* and plucks the strings (pizzicato). In essence, the strikingly original, brief third movement consists of an organ-style chorale stated by the piano, an impassioned, rhythmically free recitative (music that imitates the natural rhythms and inflections of speech) for the cello, and then a remarkable synthesis or combination of the two. The last movement provides a stunning conclusion, albeit one that is a mite too facile and glib with its salon-type piano part.

Organ Sonatas

While Mendelssohn was on a concert tour of England in 1844, a publisher asked him to compose a set of six organ pieces. At first Mendelssohn called them voluntaries, an English term that is vaguely defined as organ works to be played in church as an adjunct to the service. Mendelssohn later changed the title to sonatas, even though they are mostly cycles of related but independent pieces typical of the organ repertoire—preludes, fugues, variations, and chorale fantasies—rather than the sequence of movements usually found in sonatas.

Many consider the **Sonata for Organ No. 1 in F minor, Op. 65, No. 1,** among Mendelssohn's best efforts in the form. The first movement alternates the development of the chorale "Ich hab' in Gottes Herz und Sinn" with fugal sections. A slow movement follows, somewhat similar in style to Mendelssohn's *Songs Without Words,* and the work ends with an exultant, toccatalike finale.

Smaller in scale than Number 1, the **Sonata for Organ No. 2 in C minor, Op. 65, No. 2,** has four brief movements—the first introductory in nature, a delicate, contrapuntal slow movement, a processional, and a final fugue that Mendelssohn had composed in 1839 as an independent organ piece.

The **Sonata for Organ No. 3 in A, Op. 65, No. 3,** ranks with Number 1 in popularity. Of the two movements, the first looms by far over the other as the more important; after an introduction of great dignity, Mendelssohn presents a fugue to which he adds the chorale "Auf tiefer Not," played with the pedals. The pleasant, relaxed second movement presents a welcome counterbalance to the sonata's challenging opening.

The cheerful **Sonata for Organ No. 4 in B flat, Op. 65, No. 4,** makes its appeal in several ways: scintillating figures open the sonata in a succession of striking, colorful guises; the ardent third movement presents a particularly attractive lyrical flow and textual clarity; and a theme of impressive dignity precedes and follows the cleverly constructed fugue of the finale.

Among all the sonatas, the **Sonata for Organ No. 5 in D, Op. 65, No. 5,** strikes the listener as being the least unified. The first movement grows from an original chorale; the second sounds like a Venetian barcarolle; and the extended final movement bears little obvious relation to either of the two preceding sections.

The well-liked **Sonata for Organ No. 6 in D minor, Op. 65, No. 6,** seems particularly organ-specific. A very moving chorale, "Vater unser im Himmelreich," heard at the beginning, is followed by a set of variations and a fugue based on the chorale melody. The closing section develops organically from the fugue.

Wolfgang Amadeus Mozart

Born January 27, 1756, in Salzburg
Died December 5, 1791, in Vienna

THE story of Mozart's life—from immense childhood successes at the royal courts of Europe, to great difficulty in obtaining commissions and a complete inability to receive a permanent appointment as an adult (despite the succession of masterpieces that he was producing), to tragic death weeks before his thirty-sixth birthday—is too familiar to bear retelling. Yet, through it all, from age seven until two years before his death, Mozart continued writing a succession of sonatas that testifies to the sure and steady growth of his expressive abilities and the speedy development of his technical mastery.

During Mozart's lifetime, and long past his demise, his publishers seldom bothered to assign opus numbers to his music with any consistency, making it very difficult to date and organize his music in order of composition. Finally, in 1862, an Austrian musician and naturalist, Dr. Ludwig Köchel, prepared a complete thematic catalog of Mozart's music so that each piece is identified by a K (Köchel) number. In 1937, the musicologist Alfred Einstein revised and corrected Köchel's catalog in the light of more recent scholarship. A further revision—the sixth edition, prepared in 1964—is even more accurate. The works discussed below are placed in the order of the earlier, more familiar, Köchel numbers, but where the sixth edition numbers differ, they are shown in parentheses.

Piano Sonatas

According to Alfred Einstein, Mozart's piano sonatas were written for the piano, not the harpsichord or clavichord. True, the eighteenth-century piano bears only a distant kinship to today's piano, but it was closer to the modern instrument than to the keyboard instruments that preceded it. Also, Mozart wrote most of the sonatas for performance at his own concerts, not as pedagogical exercises, even though they are widely used for that purpose today.

Mozart's seventeen piano sonatas fall very neatly into three groups. The first six early sonatas were composed in 1774 and 1775—five while the composer was living in Salzburg, one in Munich. The seven middle-period sonatas were written "on the road," in either Mannheim or Paris during the years 1777 and 1778. And the four late sonatas were completed in Vienna between 1784 and 1789.

In the summer of 1774, when he was eighteen years old and employed as concertmaster of the court orchestra in Salzburg, Mozart began the composition of six piano sonatas that he planned to perform in public and to have published in one edition. Overflowing with bright, fresh musical ideas, these sonatas were particular favorites of the composer and he played them frequently.

The first four of these youthful works, the **Piano Sonata in C, K. 279 (189d)**, **Piano Sonata in F, K. 280 (189e)**, **Piano Sonata in B flat, K. 281 (189f)**, and **Piano Sonata in E flat, K. 282 (189g)**, are not as well known as the fifth, the **Piano Sonata in G, K. 283 (189h)**, which is an alluring work, graceful in its carriage and filled with a plenitude of diverse melodic materials.

The outstanding final sonata of the six, the **Piano Sonata in D, K. 284 (205b)**, was composed in March 1775 on a commission from Baron Thaddäus von Durnitz, a music lover in Munich. This fine work, forceful and ambitious, many judge to be the most magnificent of this early set.

The second and third movements of the D major sonata generate particular interest. The slow second movement, entitled Rondeau en Polonaise, follows the form of a rondo with a distinctive theme that occurs three times. Between the statements of the theme Mozart inserts contrasting episodes. The theme itself has the rhythmic character of a polonaise—a Polish national dance in three-beat time that is stately, but with some animation. The third and final movement consists of a theme with twelve variations in which Mozart exhibits what Alfred Einstein calls a "rich flow of invention." This quite bright, happy-sounding movement offers deep rewards to both performer and listener.

(Scholars have some evidence that Baron von Durnitz gave Mozart a number of suggestions on the sonata's musical content, but are not sure whether they were accepted. They also believe that the baron failed to give Mozart the monies promised upon completion of this outstanding composition.)

For a couple of years these first six sonatas fulfilled Mozart's need for music to perform in concert. But while on a leisurely tour that took him to Mannheim and Paris he felt the need for additional repertoire and, from the fall of 1777 through the summer of 1778, he composed the seven so-called middle-period sonatas.

From Mozart's letters we know a great deal about the genesis of the **Piano Sonata in C, K. 309 (284b)**. Regarding his performance of the first and third movements of the sonata in October 1777, prior to setting down the notes, he wrote to his father, "I then played all of a sudden a magnificent sonata in C major out of my head and a rondo to finish up with." Subsequent letters tell how he prepared the sonata for Rosa Cannabich, daughter of Christian Cannabich, the Kapellmeister in Mannheim, and how he worked to make the Andante "fit closely the character of Mlle. Rosa." Mozart described Rosa, age fifteen, as "a very pretty and charming girl." He went on to say, "She is very intelligent and steady for her age. She is serious, does not say much, but when she does speak she is pleasant and amiable." He then concludes, "It really is a fact. She is exactly like the Andante."

The sonata follows the standard three-movement form: the first, with its wonderfully clear formal structure, at times sounds orchestral in its conception; the second, Rosa's Andante, seems to capture the loveliness and introspective beauty of the young woman; and the finale emerges as a smoothly flowing, elegant rondo.

The **Piano Sonata in A minor, K. 310 (300d)**, a dark, tragic work, was perhaps written in reaction to the death of Mozart's mother who was with him on tour in Paris during July 1778. The key of A minor was the key of despair for Mozart, and this gloomy, dramatic sonata grips the listener in its impassioned expressivity.

The main theme of the rather slow first movement makes considerable use of the dotted (long-short) rhythm that is often associated with funeral marches. The contrasting second theme conveys a much more cantabile character. Great furies rage in the following development section before the two themes return.

Despite some consolation in the slow movement, the excitement and agitation that precede the return of the opening section rob the movement of any sense of calm or acceptance.

Deep shadows and an understated air of foreboding run through the last movement, and lead to a less than happy ending.

It seems quite obvious that Mozart conceived the **Piano Sonata in D, K. 311 (284c)**, composed in Mannheim in November 1777, as an impressive major work. The lively, exuberant first movement makes its impact on the listener both with its unusual harmonies and with the order of the themes, which are reversed when brought back in the recapitulation.

Some commentators hear in the beautifully expressive slow movement a declaration of Mozart's affection for Aloysia Weber, his first true love, even though he later married her sister.

The high point of the sonata comes in the concluding rondo, with its swinging rhythm and delightful, spontaneous touch. A point of special interest is the cadenza that is heard just before the last return of the principal subject.

The ever joyful **Piano Sonata in C, K. 330 (300h)**, stands as a sound refutation to those who falsely associate melancholy with quality, and gaiety with triviality. From the bright clarity of the first movement, which includes cheerful bird calls, through the intimate loveliness of the songlike Andante, to the ebullience and brilliance of the Allegretto, this sonata continually radiates delightful good feelings—and yet belongs in the company of the very finest essays in the form.

The **Piano Sonata in A, K. 331 (300i)**, also from the summer of 1778, scores high marks as Mozart's best-known piano sonata. Pianist Vladimir Horowitz called it "the apotheosis of gallantry and grace," yet it is perhaps the least representative sonata from the viewpoint of formal structure. Imagine, a three-movement sonata and not one movement in sonata form.

The restrained, intimate first movement consists of a theme and six variations. The movement evolves from a simple theme that Mozart decorates and ornaments, without ever straying very far from the original melody.

Instead of a slow movement, Mozart proceeds to a Menuetto. The middle section, or Trio, has a broad theme that, in a way, manages to take the place of a slow movement.

The popular, marchlike last movement, the Alla turca ("In the Turkish style"), captures the high spirits of the Janissary bands' music with their prominent cymbals, triangles, and drums.

Mozart completed two other sonatas in Paris during the summer of 1778—the **Piano Sonata in F, K. 332 (300k)**, and **Piano Sonata in B flat, K. 333 (315c)**. Most pianists find the first a grateful piece, with an outstanding final movement that is so richly and imaginatively written that it can be considered a herald of the approaching Romantic era. The K. 333 finds Mozart reaching a new, and even higher level of lyricism. The masterly second movement, Andante cantabile, can easily take its rightful place among his most mature works. The writing style of the last movement so closely resembles that of a concerto that one seems to hear solo piano passages alternating with the massed sound of orchestral tuttis and there is even a cadenza to heighten the illusion.

Mozart's life and music underwent major changes in the years from 1778, which marked the end of his middle-period sonatas, and 1784, when he started his late sonatas. Perhaps most important, he left the employ of the Archbishop of Salzburg in 1781, with the famous kick in the backside, and struck out on his own.

Mozart's income, albeit very low, came primarily from giving "academies," programs of his own music, each one usually featuring a new piano concerto, along with miscellaneous smaller works, which he composed and performed. Contemporary accounts indicate that he was presenting as many as twenty academies a year in Vienna. His marriage in 1782 and the death of his father five years later also brought about major upheavals in his personal life.

During this period, Mozart came to know the music of Bach and other Baroque masters, and adapted their use of counterpoint and polyphony to his own musical needs. He accomplished a new and more convincing blending of the *galant*—the light, elegant style of the Rococo—with the "learned" approach, which included greater use of counterpoint, logical, well-ordered formal structures, and an emphasis on clarity of melody, harmony, and rhythm. At the same time, he achieved in his music a greater depth of expression and level of craftsmanship, increased confidence, and a surer technical skill.

Of the **Piano Sonata in C minor, K. 457,** Ludwig Köchel wrote in his catalog of Mozart's music, "Without question this is the most important of all Mozart's piano sonatas." It is indeed a mighty work, but one whose grandeur and passion are pervaded by a feeling of tragic pain and anguish. Unlike the despair portrayed in Mozart's earlier A minor sonata (K. 310), the C minor sonata cries out most pathetically—in a way that Mozart seemed to associate with this particular key.

The sonata opens with a forceful rising figure in unison that impresses with its drive and energy. The second subject can be heard as a dialogue between a high and a low voice. Intense and somber, the movement packs a great emotional impact within its compact length.

After the storminess of the Allegro, the Adagio is still somewhat clouded over, but with a certain tender tranquillity that offers calmness and consolation after all the agitation. Mozart makes sure to vary and ornament the main melody for each of its repetitions in this rondo-form movement.

The finale sees the return of the opening movement's tragic character. One device that Mozart uses with telling effect involves starting a dialogue between two voices, which he then suddenly and abruptly interrupts with silence.

Mozart published the C minor sonata together with his Fantasia, K. 475, also in C minor. Although they were conceived as two separate pieces, linking them in publication may well be Mozart's way of suggesting that the Fantasia be played as a prelude to the sonata—an arrangement that works extremely well in recital.

The **Piano Sonata in F, K. 533-494,** a most fascinating work, may not always be listed among Mozart's sonatas because of the way it was created. On June 10, 1786, Mozart wrote a Rondo (in F, K. 494) as an instructional piece for one of his pupils. Then, on January 3, 1788, to repay a debt to a friend, the publisher Franz Hoffmeister, Mozart completed two movements, an Allegro and Andante (also in F, K. 533), to precede the Rondo and make a complete sonata, which he then presented to Hoffmeister.

Despite the strange circumstances of its composition, many regard the F major as one of Mozart's finest sonatas, with particularly outstanding use of counterpoint. The themes of the first movement are not particularly distinguished; yet as Mozart expands and develops them they become imbued with wonderful expressive qualities. The Andante, with its vaulted, arching theme, probably stands out as the best movement of the sonata because of its intense emotional quality. The large-proportioned Rondo presents four repetitions of the theme instead of the more usual three, which is understandable since it started life as a full-length composition by itself.

Mozart called his **Piano Sonata in C, K. 545,** a "little sonata for beginners." Completed on June 26, 1788, Mozart probably intended it for pedagogical purposes with one of his students. While it is easy to play and modest in length, this miniature masterpiece regrettably appears frequently on student programs where the performers may lack the maturity and insight necessary to project the work's many superb qualities. Also, because of its minimal technical demands, some virtuoso performers apply a heavy interpretative overlay to this extraordinary, but simple, piece, completely distorting the music's ingenuous charms. For its full effect to be enjoyed, this fragile work of art must be played with great purity of style and sensitivity to the composer's intentions.

The **Piano Sonata in B flat, K.** 570, which is dated February 1789, resembles the K. 545 sonata in the way its surface child-like transparency disguises the depth of its emotional content and musical meaning. Mozart scholar Alfred Einstein, a particular admirer of this piano sonata, called it "perhaps the most completely rounded of them all, the ideal of his piano sonata." In all three movements we hear Mozart merging both *galant* and learned elements to delight the ear, the heart, and the brain.

Mozart's final work in the form, the **Piano Sonata in D, K.** 576, of 1789, was the first and only completed sonata of a proposed set of six "easy" sonatas that he planned to present to Princess Frederica of Prussia in anticipation of a handsome cash gift. Although he thought of this as an "easy" sonata it is, by far, the most technically difficult of all the piano sonatas.

This outstanding sonata pulses with strength and vigor, and makes a fitting culmination to Mozart's piano sonatas. The first movement suggests the lilting swing and rhythm of hunting horns, which has led to the occasionally used subtitle "Hunt." The treatment of the theme, though, is highly contrapuntal, with much use of canon, in which the same melody is sequentially imitated by other voices.

The Adagio is best described as gemlike and exquisite. While the writing sounds perfectly idiomatic for the piano, at the same time it has some of the qualities of a florid coloratura aria.

Although Mozart wrote the last movement in a modified sonata-allegro form, he did not create a sharp contrast between the two themes. The work, therefore, gives the overall impression of monothematic construction.

Violin Sonatas

While best remembered today as a great composer, Mozart is also known as having been a phenomenal pianist, from his days as the *Wunderkind* darling of the courts of Europe to his early emergence as a mature artist. Less familiar is the fact that Mozart was equally accomplished as a violinist, playing both violin and piano concertos at his youthful appearances and later serving as concertmaster and violin soloist with the court orchestra in Salzburg. With this background, it becomes entirely understandable that he produced over his tragically short lifetime a full thirty-one violin sonatas.

Oddly enough, Mozart entitled his early works for violin "sonatas for piano with violin *ad libitum.*" The later ones were designated for piano with the accompaniment of violin, which was an advantage from the violinist's viewpoint, since now at least the violin *had* to be included!

His earliest sonatas—the four written in Paris when he was eight years old (K. 6 through 9), the six produced in London the following year, which sometimes appear with an added cello part (K. 10 through 15), and the six he composed in the Hague in 1766 (K. 26 through 31)—were essentially piano sonatas with occasional interjections, melodic imitations, and accompaniment figures for the violin. In the subsequent sonatas, though, the violin's role grew until it was the full equal of the piano—but in keeping with eighteenth-century tradition, the designation "piano and violin" stayed the same.

Mozart composed the following violin sonatas in Mannheim and Paris while on tour in 1778: the **Piano and Violin Sonata in C, K. 296, Piano and Violin Sonata in G, K. 301 (293a), Piano and Violin Sonata in E flat, K. 302 (293b), Piano and Violin Sonata in C, K. 303 (293c), Piano and Violin Sonata in E minor, K. 304 (300c), Piano and Violin Sonata in A, K. 305 (293d), and Piano and Violin Sonata in D, K. 306 (300l).**

The significance of these sonatas is partly historic; they are the first to give the violin a role of both substance and importance. Of the seven sonatas, the E minor, K. 304, is by far the most amazing, what Alfred Einstein calls a "miracle." Somehow the twenty-two-year-old composer was able to plumb the depths of human emotion and produce a work that vibrates with passion and drama. Since the E minor was composed during the summer of 1778, when his mother died while with him in Paris, Mozart may have used it to express some of the anguish he felt at her death.

The two-movement sonata provides an illuminating study in

classical restraint. Starting from the stark unison of the opening, the sonata seems to be smoldering with raging fires that are banked and held under tight control by the traditions of eighteenth-century compositional style. The Tempo de Menuetto that follows is much more peaceful and contemplative, but nonetheless penetrated with pain and pathos.

The next set of sonatas—the **Piano and Violin Sonata in F, K. 376 (374d)**, **Piano and Violin Sonata in F, K. 377 (374e)**, **Piano and Violin Sonata in B flat, K. 378 (317d)**, **Piano and Violin Sonata in G, K. 379 (373a)**, and **Piano and Violin Sonata in E flat, K. 380 (374f)**—were all composed in Vienna between April and June 1781, with the exception of K. 378, which was written two years earlier. In all of them, Mozart shows a greater maturity of style—less under the influence of other composers, more concise, and with a richer, closer relationship between the two instruments.

The most frequently performed of this group of six sonatas is K. 378, in B flat, one of Mozart's major works. Particularly distinguished by its continual flow of inspiration, the sonata opens with a meltingly beautiful theme, which is followed by a cornucopia of melodic largess; phrase after phrase effortlessly pours forth with reassuring abundance and richness.

Mozart presents two basic ideas in the second movement—the first is light, bright, and sunny; the second, dark and somewhat mysterious. By simply alternating the two sections he creates a wonderfully effective movement.

Sparkling with high spirits and good cheer, the finale, a rondo, provides an impressive conclusion to the entire sonata.

Information on many of Mozart's sonatas can be hard to come by. But a letter he wrote concerning his sonata in G, K. 379, gives interesting insights into his composing style. The letter, dated April 8, 1781, and addressed to his father, describes how he had played the piano part to his new piano and violin sonata at a concert earlier that day. He indicates that he composed the sonata, which we believe to be K. 379, "last night between eleven and twelve"!

Although written in such great haste, it contains a most inspiring first movement, which opens with a long, powerful slow introduction that almost qualifies as a movement on its own. In the fast body of the movement the two instruments receive equal treatment, interacting in an impassioned dialogue.

Mozart ends the sonata with a theme and five variations. The tranquillity that pervades this movement should not be construed as indifference or lack of personal involvement.

The last three Mozart violin sonatas, by far his finest works for the two instruments, fall into a separate group. When Mozart and the young Italian violinist Regina Strinasacchi, gave the premiere of the first of the three, the **Piano and Violin Sonata in B flat, K. 454,** in Vienna on April 29, 1784, Emperor Joseph was in attendance. After the concert, the emperor summoned Mozart to the royal box and asked that he bring along the piano part to the sonata. The emperor commented that he had not observed Mozart so much as glance at the music during the performance. In response, Mozart opened the score and showed that he had, in fact, played from a blank sheet of music paper! Since he had not had time to write it out, he explained, he had just played the piano part from memory.

Composed primarily for professional performers rather than amateurs like most of his other sonatas, the K. 454 impresses with its virtuosity. The very dignified Largo introduction to the first movement flows along in a majestic stream; the two instruments are treated equitably, each making its own independent contribution to the total musical fabric.

The Andante suggests a freedom of approach that perhaps can best be described as rhapsodic. The violin writing deserves particular mention for its remarkable blend of the seemingly opposite traits of intimacy and virtuosity.

Although the finale has a somewhat inward-looking, introspective air, its geniality and many melodic surprises prevent any slide into the maudlin or sentimental.

Mozart composed the **Piano and Violin Sonata in E flat, K. 481,** the second of his three great last-period sonatas, in 1785, while working on his operatic masterpiece *The Marriage of Figaro.* The first movement, although generally restrained and somewhat austere, creates a rich interplay between the two instruments. The Adagio emerges as the emotional center of the sonata; it is a profound, deeply felt movement. In the finale, a theme and six variations, the composer assigns the burden of the music to the piano, relegating the violin to a rather more supportive role.

The Köchel-Einstein catalog of Mozart's music calls the **Piano and Violin Sonata in A, K. 526,** the "most significant of the keyboard violin sonatas of Mozart." Completed on August 24, 1787, K. 526 is the final sonata, except for the rather slight K. 547 of 1788, which exists more as an instructional sonatina than as a full-scale sonata. The layout for the K. 526 conforms to a grand plan—one that maintains a perfect balance between violin and piano, between the surface beauties of the *galant* and the intellectual rigors of the learned style, and between beautiful singing melodies and complex contrapuntal weavings.

Assorted rhythmic piquancies enliven the characteristically robust and high-speed Molto allegro opening movement. A good measure of drama and passion infuse the writing, but always confined within the bounds of eighteenth-century instrumental practices. One is continually aware of Mozart's evenhandedness, giving both instruments a go at the themes and in general dividing equitably the opportunities as leading melodic voice.

While the texture of the Andante tends to be spare and thin, the harmonies emerge full bodied and rich. The strong motion of this profound movement propels it forward, as one instrument or the other almost continually plays a flowing eighth-note figure.

The absolutely joyous Presto combines little jazzy rhythms and turns of phrase with elements of moto perpetuo, and provides a wonderfully high-spirited conclusion both to this sonata and to the entire series of Mozart's sonatas for these instruments.

Francis Poulenc

Born January 7, 1899, in Paris
Died January 30, 1963, in Paris

IN the years after World War I, a number of French composers reacted against the Impressionism of Debussy and Ravel, as well as the Romantic and Expressionist trends in German music. These composers were bound together by a number of shared musical goals: to keep their compositions simple and clear; to make light, sophisticated melodies the primary component of their writing; and to approach everything in a spirit of good fun and humor. They enjoyed shocking listeners with jarring dissonances and unexpected rhythms and often sought inspiration in the "real world" of pop songs, jazz, and the music of the café and music hall.

This informal, loosely organized group of French composers—Louis Durcy, Arthur Honegger, Darius Milhaud, Germaine Tailleferre, Georges Auric, and Francis Poulenc—came to be called Les Six. Poulenc was probably the most impudent and saucy memeber of this ad-hoc association. And his early sonatas offer many delightful examples of the tongue-in-cheek style they all sought to achieve.

Poulenc's sonatas divide themselves very neatly into three discrete groups, the first of which contains the **Sonata for Two Clarinets** (1918), **Sonata for Piano Four Hands** (1918), and **Sonata for Clarinet and Bassoon** (1922). The composer commented that the two wind sonatas "maintain a certain youthful vitality," a description that applies to the keyboard sonata as well. Brash and flippant in character, all three surprise with their "wrong note" dissonances, much like disobedient children poking fun at their musical elders. The shared features of these sonatas are their brevity and their three-movement structure—Fast, Slow, Fast. Each movement is organized into either a modified three-part (ABA) or rondo (ABACA) form, and depends for its effect on much repetition of a few brief motifs. The fast movements sound particularly lighthearted and tuneful; the slow ones tend to be melancholy, sometimes verging on the sentimental. All three sonatas are performed today in revisions prepared by Poulenc.

Even though Poulenc once said, "I have always adored wind instruments, preferring them to strings," he wrote two sonatas for string players, the **Sonata for Violin and Piano** (1943) and **Sonata for Cello and Piano** (1948). In a letter, Poulenc said of his violin sonata, "A proper balance of sound between violin and piano can only be obtained by treating them equally. The prima donna violin above an arpeggiated piano makes me vomit."

The Violin Sonata does indeed keep both instruments on a par; the only exception is a short passage for piano alone. In the three-part first movement a slightly slower middle section comes between the statement and the free repeat of the opening. The small-scaled, modest second movement serves as a lyrical intermezzo separating the two fast movements. Titled Presto tragico, the finale startles by inserting pop-style music-hall tunes into the rather somber prevailing tone.

Poulenc began making sketches for the Cello Sonata in 1940, but abandoned the project for several years, until he was newly inspired by the playing of the renowned French cello virtuoso Pierre Fournier. The sonata, which was completed in October 1948, is much more romantic than the earlier sonatas and projects a much greater personal involvement. The only sonata in four movements, it starts with a typically sparkling Poulenc opener, goes on to a singing, poetic contrast for the second movement, which is followed by a sprightly scherzo. A lengthy final movement, not unlike the first, ends the work.

Composed in 1953, and therefore chronologically part of the last group of sonatas, the **Sonata for Two Pianos** actually stands alone as an extremely serious work, with no thought to please, shock, or amuse. A difficult, intricate piece with many acerbic dissonances, it was written under the influence of Stravinsky in a Neoclassical style. The sonata assumes an arch shape, starting with an introductory Prologue and a scherzolike Allegro molto, both of which build to the Andante, the movement Poulenc described as "a lyric, profound outpouring." The Epilogue, in the composer's words, "is not a Finale, but a recapitulation of the other three movements, preceded by a new theme."

The final three sonatas, for flute, clarinet, and oboe (at his death Poulenc was planning a bassoon sonata to complete the set of four woodwinds), are among Poulenc's finest compositions. These works find him at a new and even higher level of maturity and musical mastery. The sonatas are fully as tuneful and enchanting as the earlier ones, but in addition they radiate a confidence and serenity that was not before apparent.

Poulenc composed the **Sonata for Flute and Piano** from December 1956 to March 1957, right after completing his opera *Dialogues des Carmélites,* and included in the sonata several melodies borrowed from the opera. A few years later, during the summer of 1962, Poulenc wrote the **Sonata for Clarinet and Piano,** which shares a number of traits with the earlier Flute Sonata. The first movements of both works have a melancholy cast, and a relaxed and leisurely tempo. After warm, gentle slow movements, the rousing high spirits of the finales provide strong, positive endings.

Poulenc's last sonata and final composition, the **Sonata for Oboe and Piano,** followed the Clarinet Sonata in the summer of 1962; but for a few reasons it stands apart from both the clarinet and flute sonatas. Its arrangement of movements—Slow, Fast, Slow—differs from the others, and its quality of resignation and contentment is unique in Poulenc's sonatas. The music bespeaks a man at peace with himself, comfortable with his religious beliefs, and content with his accomplishments as a human being and as a creative artist. In the three-part first movement, "Elégie," the nervous middle section provides a sharp contrast to the several calm, quiet motifs that the composer introduces at the beginning and freely repeats at the end. The second movement—a gay scherzo—sounds more like a typical Poulenc finale.

The concluding movement, "Déploration," proves to be the last music Poulenc ever wrote. Described by the composer as "a sort of liturgical chant," it provides a final glimpse of Poulenc in a highly emotional, reflective light.

Sergei Prokofiev

Born April 23, 1891, in Sontsovka, Russia
Died March 5, 1953, in Moscow

IN 1941 Prokofiev prepared a brief autobiographical sketch for the festivities celebrating his fiftieth birthday. The account detailed the five major stylistic tendencies he detected in his music: Classicism, innovation, motor element, lyricism, and the grotesque (which includes, in his words, "jest, laughter, and mockery"). All these elements can be heard, to greater or lesser extent, in his fifteen instrumental sonatas.

On the first page of the **Sonata for Cello and Piano, Op. 119**, Prokofiev quotes a familiar line by the well-known Russian writer Maxim Gorky: "Man—that was a proud sound." The music, with its optimism and outgoing good humor, does indeed appear to be a glorification of human existence. Prokofiev began the sonata in 1947 and completed it two years later, guided by suggestions from cellist Mstislav Rostropovich to help him write idiomatically for the instrument.

The sonata opens with a slightly mysterious theme, illuminated with some flashes of Prokofiev's wit, to be followed by a doleful and morose subsidiary subject. The movement unfolds in traditional sonata-allegro form, but with both themes taking on an ingenuous, folksong, fairy tale quality, as Prokofiev works them out. The scherzo, which comes next, consists of a light, carefree opening, succeeded by romantic music for the central section, and a return of the first part. The fast last movement, including a quotation of the sonata's opening theme, features two contrasting melodies—the first a singing, cantabile line, the second a humorous, mocking dancelike tune.

In June 1943, in the midst of World War II, Prokofiev left Moscow and moved for several months to the city of Perm in the Ural Mountains where he worked simultaneously on three major scores—the ballet *Cinderella,* the opera *War and Peace,* and music for the film *Ivan the Terrible.* Almost as a diversion from these monumental undertakings, and inspired by the playing of the French flutist Georges Barrère, Prokofiev started his **Sonata for Flute and Piano, Op.** 94, a task he described as "perhaps inappropriate at the moment, but pleasant." Prokofiev further explained that he wrote the sonata because "this instrument had for a long time attracted me and it seemed to me that it was little represented in the musical literature. I wanted this Sonata to have a classical, clear, transparent sonority."

Many regard the cheerful Flute Sonata as the happiest composition that Prokofiev produced during the war years. Charming and graceful, it is endowed with great élan and energy. The two subjects in the sonata-allegro first movement make their appeal simply and directly; the poised main theme, heard at the outset, sounds vocal in character, while the subsidiary theme makes a somewhat more rhythmic impression. The short development section starts with a mock military march. An almost exact recapitulation of the themes and a short coda round off the movement.

The piquant, mischievous Scherzo sparkles with incisive rhythmic interplay between the flute and piano. The vivacity is replaced by a warm glow in the middle section, with its pensive, contemplative melody. A return of the opening marks the end of the movement.

The beginning of the short Andante movement sounds disarmingly simple and lyrical in style. In the middle the music grows busier and a bit more agitated. The last part returns to the mood of the opening—except for the piano playing little flurries of rushing notes, remnants from the just concluded middle section.

Stormy and boisterous, the rondo finale bursts forth in a brilliant display of musical pyrotechnics—Prokofiev at his exciting best. Once the energy is spent, the piano starts an interlude that sounds like a mocking version of one of the notorious Hanon finger exercises for the instrument. A brief glimpse of the mercurial main subject comes next, followed by a cantilena section. In quick order the composer then presents the theme, a taste of Hanon, and a virtuosic final traversal of the theme.

Completed in the summer of 1943, the Flute Sonata received its premiere in Moscow on December 7 of that year.

Piano Sonatas

Prokofiev, an outstanding keyboard virtuoso in his own right, contributed more to the modern piano sonata literature, in both size and importance, than any other contemporary composer. He completed nine sonatas, left a tenth unfinished, and was planning an eleventh at the time of his death. The works maintain some ties to the past by following traditional forms and concepts of key and tonality, and by their emphasis on melody. They are, nonetheless, highly imaginative, innovative works, characteristic of the twentieth century in their frequent use of jarring, dissonant harmonies and complex, shifting rhythms, and in their exploration of new and novel piano sonorities.

Although the **Piano Sonata No. 1 in F minor, Op. 1,** and **Piano Sonata No. 2 in D minor, Op. 14,** were both begun in 1907, while Prokofiev was still a student at the St. Petersburg Conservatory, they evolved in opposite ways. With the F minor sonata, Prokofiev started with three movements, dropped the second and third movements, and revised and expanded the first, issuing it finally in 1909 as a richly romantic one-movement composition. The 1912 D minor sonata began as a one-movement sonatina, to which Prokofiev added a scherzo he had written for a class assignment, plus two more movements that he composed specifically for the purpose, creating, in the end, a full four-movement sonata. Instead of looking back to nineteenth-century practices, though, the second sonata anticipates the mature Prokofiev, with clear, energetic melodies, sharp dissonances, and lively, playful rhythms.

Finished in 1917, the **Piano Sonata No. 3 in A minor, Op.**

28, and **Piano Sonata No. 4 in C minor, Op.** 29, nevertheless
are based on music Prokofiev wrote during his student days in
1907 and 1908. For that reason they are sometimes subtitled
"From Old Notebooks."

Listeners and players alike enjoy the one-movement Third Sonata, a fiery and dramatic display piece. Although based on a
youthful sonata, Prokofiev made comparatively few changes
when preparing the final version. Generally speaking, he kept
the same themes and general outline, but sharpened some of the
harmonies and pointed up the piano writing into a more virtuosic, bravura style. Structured in overall sonata-allegro form, the
sonata begins with a powerful opening theme distinguished by
wide leaps, erratic rhythmic patterns, and shocking dissonances.
The second theme, simple, subdued, and very moving, furnishes
a stark contrast. The development, which is mostly concerned
with the first theme, opens and closes with great strength. The
free recapitulation omits the by now familiar first theme and
brings back only the second theme, although much altered.

Considerably more thoughtful, restrained, and contemplative,
the Fourth Sonata presents a very different facet of Prokofiev's
musical personality. A substantial work in three movements, it
includes sections of languorous melancholy that alternate with
passages of energetic vigor. Two themes—a strong, epic melody
and one that is more narrative and slightly humorous—dominate
the first movement. The outstanding Andante in three-part form
sets out with grace and majesty, proceeds to a middle section
that is gentle and lyrical, and combines the two sections to conclude the movement. Buoyant and exuberant, the joyful rondo
finale sings out its optimistic, life-asserting message in ringing
tones.

Perhaps the reason the **Piano Sonata No. 5 in C, Op. 38,** of
1923 has not found much favor with modern audiences is that
the saucy insolence heard in the earlier works has been replaced
in part by rather cold, cerebral formulations. But the highly attractive opening movement usually delights listeners with its
fresh, charming main subject and a contrast that sounds like a
musical description of some somber, grotesque creature from
ancient Russian myth. Best categorized as a slow scherzo, the

second movement has a sort of waltzlike feel, albeit tinged with irony and sarcasm. The highly complex third movement, the most intellectual and challenging part of the sonata, ventures at times into bitonality, with each hand playing in a different key.

Nearly thirty years after completing the Fifth Sonata, Prokofiev himself declared it was too "intricate," and in 1952 prepared a simplified version, which he published as Op. 135.

Prokofiev's composing in the second half of 1939 was shaped by two influences—the overwhelming disruption caused by the outbreak of World War II in September and, on a more personal level, his discovery of Romain Rolland's monumental and highly romanticized biography of Beethoven. At the time Prokofiev simultaneously began preparing sketches for the **Piano Sonata No. 6 in A, Op. 82, Piano Sonata No. 7 in B flat, Op. 83,** and **Piano Sonata No. 8 in B flat, Op. 84,** flitting back and forth in his composing from sonata to sonata. He completed the Sixth Sonata in 1940, but the others were not done until 1942 and 1944, respectively. Composed against a background of fighting and bloodshed, the three sonatas are sometimes grouped together as the "War Sonatas"; in them many hear the harshness and brutality of battle, the heroism of the soldiers, and the touches of love and tenderness that become even more precious amid the horrors and destruction of a world at war.

The Sixth Sonata reveals all the power, iconoclasm, and profound lyricism of Prokofiev's earlier works, but with a new maturity and intensity of expression. Its stern opening immediately conjures up visions of armies in battle, while the contrasting theme, a rambling, melancholy melody, somehow seems bereft of all emotion. The development, after its motoric start, whips up to a furious climax that requires the pianist to play *glissandi* (sliding from note to note) and *con pugno* (striking the keys "with the fist"). After an abbreviated recapitulation, Prokofiev again calls forth the furies in the concluding coda. A respite is needed after this onslaught, and Prokofiev provides one in the Allegretto, a gay, dancing movement of sparkling delight. By contrast, the extended third movement appears slow, thickly textured, and earthbound. At its outset, the last movement sounds like a playful, amusing conclusion to the sonata, but near the end it changes its character and becomes dark and sinister as it quotes the opening theme of the first movement. The lighthearted tunes of the finale come back, but they too take on somewhat frightening hues, leading to a flashy, but joyless, ending.

Prokofiev provided a succinct description of the Seventh Sonata: "The first movement unfolds in fairly rapid tempo; the second is a lyrical andante, at one moment tender, at another tense; the finale is in 7/8." The two themes of the first movement resemble in character, though not in notes, the parallel themes in the Sixth Sonata: the first severe, the second sad and ghostly. A rich and sonorous melody, suggesting peace and tranquillity, opens the second movement. In time the melody gives way to another theme, its remote, austere singing line floating above a foundation of highly dissonant chords. When the first theme returns it is much shortened, as though its beauty had been diminished by the anguish of the second section. The final movement, in the awkward 7/8 meter, splendidly exhibits Prokofiev's motoric tendencies, relentlessly speeding along in an almost hypnotic flow.

Dedicated to Mira Mendelson, the young woman Prokofiev met during the summer of 1939 and later married, the Eighth Sonata is much more intimate and reflective; the mood is "primarily lyrical," in the composer's words. The two themes of the first movement, one touched by melancholy and yearning, the other more nervous and brittle, become increasingly coarse during the movement's stormy development section; after the return of the themes, the grim coda reverts to the character of the development. Marked Andante sognando ("Slow, dreamy"), the peaceful and relaxed second movement contains echoes of a graceful old minuet. The whirling rhythms of the finale, basically fast and motoric throughout, are interrupted for a highly dramatic, heroic-sounding middle section, after which Prokofiev brings back the first movement's second theme and then races off to a jubilant conclusion.

The **Piano Sonata No. 9 in C, Op. 103,** may be regarded as the most reserved and individual composition of the entire group, completely lacking the shocking elements and dramatic conflicts of Prokofiev's earlier works. Not one to give up its secrets easily, the Ninth (and last) Sonata has long puzzled listeners; one indication of its poor reception is the fact that, although completed in 1947, it was not premiered until 1951 and had to wait four more years for publication. The first movement, modest and miniature in a narrative, meditative style, appeals more with its introspective poignancy than with any startling effects. The first part of the scherzo second movement is built on racing ascending and descending runs and a mocking march; it is followed by a beautiful chromatic melody in the second section, and the movement finishes with a return of the opening character. The Andante tranquillo makes a big impression by having the songlike melody alternate with a vivacious, ebullient contrast. As though bidding farewell to the piano sonata form, Prokofiev ends the predominantly lively and spirited last movement with a section marked *lontano* ("distant") in which the piano imitates the tolling of faraway bells.

Violin Sonatas

Prokofiev's sonatas for violin include two with piano, one for solo violin, and one for two violins. The **Sonata for Violin and Piano No. 1 in F minor, Op. 80,** was in part inspired by the great Russian violinist and dedicatee of the piece, David Oistrakh, and in part by the D major Handel violin sonata with which Prokofiev became familiar in the summer of 1938. The first meeting of Prokofiev and Oistrakh in 1927 gives some insight into Prokofiev's personality. At a concert in the composer's honor, Oistrakh was playing a movement of Prokofiev's First Violin Concerto. In the middle of the performance, Prokofiev leaped up from his front-row seat, shouting "No! That's not the way to play it, young man," and, sitting down at the piano, gave the eighteen-year-old violinist a humiliating public lesson. The experience apparently did little to sour relations because later the two men became very good friends and enthusiastic chess rivals.

After beginning the Violin Sonata No. 1 in 1938, Prokofiev set the dark, gloomy, "serious in mood" (Prokofiev's words) music aside, not finishing it until 1946. "The first movement,

Andante assai, is of grim character and serves as an extended introduction to the Allegro, which is in sonata form," Prokofiev wrote. Most of the important melodic strains occur in the lower register of the piano with comments by the violin. For one especially eerie section the composer directs the violinist to sound like "wind in a graveyard." "The second movement is exuberant and vigorous, but with a broader secondary theme," continued Prokofiev. In contrast to its sharp-edged rhythmic sections, Prokofiev introduced a stirring legato melody marked *eroico* ("heroic"). Evocative of a dark night with hints of the magical and supernatural, the third movement presents a quiet, atmospheric interlude between the driving second and wild fourth movements. Prokofiev described the finale as "impetuous and written in complex time," and the supercharged, high-energy movement does indeed bristle with constantly changing meters. A reprise of the "wind in a graveyard" leads to a completely unexpected quiet ending.

Present in the audience for the 1943 premiere of Prokofiev's flute sonata was David Oistrakh, who immediately accosted Prokofiev and insisted that the sonata would "enjoy a more full-blooded life on the stage" if it were transcribed for violin and piano. Prokofiev agreed, and with Oistrakh's help made a few adjustments in the flute part to make it suitable for the violin, but without altering the piano writing at all. Oistrakh and Lev Oborin then gave the first performance in Moscow of what was entitled **Sonata for Violin and Piano No. 2 in D, Op. 94a (or 94bis)** on June 17, 1944. Since then the work has won a prominent place in the repertoire, both in its original form for flute and in the violin transcription. (See pages 146–47 for discussion.)

A favorite pedagogical device of Russian string teachers was forming a group of ten to thirty students to learn one piece and perform it in unison. This practice inspired Prokofiev, in 1947, to compose a work to be played by such an assemblage; it was subsequently published as **Sonata for Solo Violin in D, Op. 115.** A work in three brief movements, the first contains a wonderful accordionlike subsidiary theme, the second weaves a set of variations on a folklike theme, and the third captures the spirit and rhythm of a rousing mazurka.

The genesis of the **Sonata for Two Violins in C, Op. 56,** dates back to the spring of 1922 when Prokofiev sat on a jury for a composition contest in Paris and listened to a very poorly written sonata for two violins. "Sometimes hearing bad compositions," Prokofiev later said, "gives birth to good ideas. One begins to think: that's not how it should be done, what's needed is this or that." Prokofiev created his contribution to the meager repertoire for two violins later that year, writing a short, modest work that maintains its restrained, remote air throughout.

Sergei Rachmaninoff

Born March 20, 1873, in Semyonovo, Russia
Died March 28, 1943, in Los Angeles

AFTER his First Symphony was introduced in 1897 Sergei Rachmaninoff endured several extremely difficult years. The symphony's premiere was an absolute disaster; the orchestra performed abominably, and the critics were merciless in their castigation of the twenty-four-year-old composer. The experience caused the already tense and nervous Rachmaninoff (Stravinsky once called him a "6½-foot scowl") to lose all confidence in his artistic ability and professional judgment.

As a consequence of this extremely unfortunate experience, Rachmaninoff became extremely depressed—some say he suffered a nervous breakdown—and he was left virtually incapable of writing music. Early in 1900, the composer began a course of treatment with psychologist Dr. Nicholai Dahl, in which the therapist used a form of autohypnotism to restore Rachmaninoff's self-assurance and motivation to compose.

The first measure of Dr. Dahl's success was the outstanding Second Piano Concerto, which Rachmaninoff wrote the following year, and which proved to be an immense success. Right after completing the concerto in April 1901, Rachmaninoff began his **Sonata for Cello and Piano in G minor, Op. 19.** The composer dated the manuscript December 12, 1901, and dedicated it to his friend Anatoly Brandukov, with whom Rachmaninoff gave the first performance in Moscow.

Dark and moody in character, the Cello Sonata is the equal of Rachmaninoff's beloved piano concerto in terms of melodic appeal, passion, and intensity of expression. The main criticism has always been that the sonata's exceedingly strong piano part can easily swallow up the cello—unless the pianist exercises particular care and restraint when the two instruments are playing together.

After a short, slow introduction, built on a rising two-note figure, the moderately paced body of the first movement begins with a lovely songlike theme that seems to grow from the introductory gesture. A series of repeated notes in the piano leads to the second subject, a soulful melody introduced by the piano and then taken up by the cello. The remainder of the movement, following a modified sonata-allegro scheme, works through and restates the two contrasting themes.

An extremely demanding movement for the cello, the allegro scherzando starts off with high-speed scurrying notes in both instruments, which are interrupted by snatches of lyrical melody for the cello. Near the middle both instruments build up to a forceful climax and then a very brief piano cadenza acts as a transition to the return of the opening section.

In the slow third movement Rachmaninoff seems to be expressing his innermost thoughts and feelings as the sounds of the two instruments merge in this most moving example of intimate, introspective music making.

The strength and vigor with which the Allegro mosso opens immediately dispels the earlier languor. Despite some residual traces of gloom from earlier movements, we are left with the distinct impression that the positive life force ultimately triumphs.

During his lifetime, Rachmaninoff was perhaps better known as a piano virtuoso than as a composer. The fact that he was so deeply involved with his performing career could not help but influence every note he wrote and might well explain the high-powered piano part he composed for the Cello Sonata. His mastery of and love for the piano also played an even greater role in inspiring and shaping the two sonatas that he wrote for that instrument. From January to May 1907, while living in Dresden, Rachmaninoff composed his **Piano Sonata No. 1, Op. 28.** In an early mention of the sonata he said that the three movements would show "three contrasting types from a literary work." Scholars believe that the work was Goethe's *Faust,* and that the three movements were musical depictions of Faust, Gretchen, and Mephistopheles. The composer abandoned the literary allusions, however, while working on the piece, and the sonata serves as a fine example of absolute music.

On completing the sonata, Rachmaninoff predicted, "Nobody will ever play this composition, it's too difficult and long." Unfortunately, even though he frequently included it on recital programs, the prophecy has been largely fulfilled.

Rachmaninoff set to work on his pivotal **Piano Sonata No. 2, Op. 36,** in 1913, largely because he was frequently asked to play concerts of his own compositions and he needed a major work for these programs. A monumental creation, the sonata carried forward the Romantic tradition of piano writing that Rachmaninoff had inherited from Beethoven, Chopin, and Liszt.

After several years of performing the Second Sonata, Rachmaninoff began to feel that the work was perhaps too massive, and in 1931 he prepared a revision that was considerably shorter and that simplified some of the more difficult and complex sections. The revision met a mixed reception; some approved, some objected, and some, like Vladimir Horowitz, believed that the best solution was an amalgam of the two versions—which Horowitz ultimately prepared and which Rachmaninoff accepted.

The extremely difficult and demanding Second Sonata is cast in three movements. The first adheres rather closely to standard sonata-allegro form. The second movement serves a double purpose; in part it is the traditional slow movement found in most sonatas, and as such is highly attractive, reflective, and poignant, rising to one stunning climax. But because it is quite brief, it also functions to some extent as an intermezzo, a transition linking the two fast movements. The finale, which some hear as the struggle between man and his fate, offers up a positive and assertive message that carries on to a bright concluding coda.

Maurice Ravel

Born March 7, 1875, in Ciboure, France
Died December 28, 1937, in Paris

FOR ease of classification, Ravel is often cited, along with Debussy, as an example of an Impressionistic composer. While a few of Ravel's orchestral works do show the concern for atmosphere, tone color, subtle textures, and fluid rhythm bordering on the improvisatory that characterize Impressionism in music, many compositions, including his sonatas, differ greatly in style and concept. This other side of Ravel's musical personality inclines toward precision and elegance; it shows an almost Neoclassical detachment and lack of intense personal involvement, while emphasizing clear, logically ordered, and well-crafted structural organization.

Ravel composed a total of four sonatas. The first, which dates back to 1897, is a sonata for violin and piano that the composer refused to submit for publication since he considered it a juvenile work. The earliest such composition he did agree to publish was his **Sonatine for Piano** of 1905.

This piece began as an entry in a composition contest for a one-movement work sponsored by the Anglo-French arts magazine *Weekly Critical Review*. Ravel's submission, however, was never brought before the judges for two reasons: the magazine was tottering on the brink of bankruptcy and Ravel was the only contestant who had entered.

Despite this inauspicious beginning, Ravel took the single movement he had written and added two more to complete the sonatine. Because the original first movement was quite short, in conformity with the contest's limit of a maximum of seventy-five measures (though Ravel's ran to seventy-seven), he kept the entire sonatine within modest dimensions to maintain the proper balance and proportion. Though small-scaled, the sonatine ranks as a major work because of its elegant style, Classical clarity, and the absolute perfection of its craftsmanship.

The first movement, which is moderate in tempo and quite passionate in temperament, follows sonata-allegro form. Melodically, though, the movement is dominated by the interval of a descending fourth, which appears in each of the subsequent movements. Played in the rhythm of a minuet, the second movement has an archaic flavor that springs, in part, from its use of modal, rather than major or minor, scales. The third movement, Animé, a free sonata-allegro, resembles perpetual motion with its unceasing rapid flow of notes. While it projects the animation Ravel calls for, the impulse seems to come more from a sort of nervous energy than from a healthy impetuosity.

Composed from 1920 to 1922, and dedicated to the memory of Claude Debussy, the **Sonata for Violin and Cello** was a "turning point in the evolution of my career," said Ravel. With this composition he veered away from the lush, opulent harmonies he had been using and turned instead to melody, quite often harsh, stark, and uncompromising melody, to carry the expressive burden of his music. "The reduction to essentials is carried to extremes," he wrote. "The fascination of harmony is rejected. There is a more and more marked reaction in the direction of melody."

Work on the sonata did not go easily; it took Ravel nearly eighteen months to complete the composition. The main theme of the Allegro, which is stated at the outset by the cello, has a cantilena flow, but with a modal feel to the melody; the subsidiary subject is pure lyricism. After a lengthy development of this material, Ravel ends the movement with a very free recapitulation.

The lively and sharply biting Scherzo sometimes moves into bitonality, in which the violin plays in one key while the cello stays in another key. The alternation of arco (bowed) and pizzicato (plucked) passages gives the movement a particular incisive bite.

All is calm and serene as the third movement starts, but the two instruments soon loudly and noisily raise their voices. In time, the vociferous squabble subsides and the movement ends just as quietly as it began.

The clamor heard in the middle of the slow movement resumes in the fast final movement as the two players engage in a musical struggle with the two themes—the first, light and nimble with frequent changes of meter; the second, colorful and rhythmic, in the style of a Hungarian folksong. But all ends well with the utterly simple consonance of the final C major chord.

Ravel carried the barebones approach of the Violin and Cello Sonata even further in the **Sonata for Violin and Piano.** He wrote that the sonata is for two "essentially incompatible instruments, which not only do not sink their differences, but accentuate the incompatibility to an even greater degree." In fact, Ravel seems to go out of his way to stress the unique tone color and sonority of each instrument, avoiding any attempt to blend together their voices.

The composer spread his work on this sonata out over four years, from 1923 to 1927. But before beginning the actual writing, Ravel commented to a friend that he had completely planned the sonata—the number of measures, the character of each of the themes and sections, even the key changes—prior to setting down one note. The first-movement themes have a bare, transparent quality that sometimes leans toward the lyrical, and sometimes delivers outbursts of sharp, short, staccato notes.

The second movement, Blues, derives from American jazz. Later, while on a tour of the United States, Ravel said, "To my mind, the 'blues' is one of your greatest musical assets, truly American despite earlier contributory influences from Africa and Spain." This highly effective movement contains the sound of the violin wailing like a saxophone, which Ravel achieves by having the violinist slide with one finger from note to note, and has the piano simulating strummed guitar chords.

Ravel begins the finale with a few introductory measures, after which the violin sets off on a difficult, high-speed, perpetual-motion chase, with the piano relegated, for the most part, to providing a simple background accompaniment.

Domenico Scarlatti

Born October 26, 1685, in Naples
Died July 23, 1757, in Madrid

FOR the first half of his life, Domenico Scarlatti was much over-shadowed by his father, Alessandro (1660–1726), the leading composer of Naples. During that time Domenico held various court positions in Italy—at Naples, Venice, and St. Peter's in Rome—and turned out any number of operas and pieces of church music that are all but forgotten today. Just before his father's death, Scarlatti accepted a position in the royal chapel in Portugal. Shortly thereafter he moved to the court of Queen Maria Barbara in Spain and it was here that he did his finest work—including the composition of approximately five hundred fifty harpsichord sonatas.

While most of the sonatas were written after 1752, when Scarlatti was fifty-seven years old, he also composed some early ones, which were published under the title *Essercizi per gravicembalo* ("Exercises for the Harpsichord") in 1738. In the preface to the *Essercizi,* Scarlatti wrote, "Do not expect any pro-found learning, but rather an ingenious jesting with art, to ac-commodate you to the mastery of the harpsichord." This remark also applies, generally speaking, to all of the subsequent sonatas. They are not calculated to provide new insights into life or to ennoble the listener, rather they are designed to provide enter-tainment and diversion, with perhaps some possibility of peda-gogical use.

Conceived much like the Chopin études, the Scarlatti sonatas are one-movement works that focus on a single technical device or a particular melodic, harmonic, or rhythmic figure, exploring its inherent musical possibilities with originality and imagination. Scarlatti seemed to approach the composition of the sonatas in a free and untrammeled way, not following any established musical laws or traditions. As the harpsichordist Ralph Kirkpatrick pointed out in his masterly study of Scarlatti, "It is almost impossible to establish rules that Scarlatti himself does not break or to define categories that he himself does not demolish."

Despite the freedom with which Scarlatti composed, and the absence of a "typical" Scarlatti sonata, many do share some common characteristics. As was mentioned, Scarlatti sonatas contain only one brief movement and are usually fast in tempo. The themes are clear, simple, short, and easily remembered. Sounding deceptively easy, the works often have very tricky passages and many examples of high-speed, dangerous, long-distance leaps. These hazards often require crossing the hands—which, curiously enough, Scarlatti himself had great difficulty in accomplishing because of his great girth.

The fact that four hundred or so of the sonatas were written out in pairs or groups of three led Kirkpatrick and others to deduce that they were meant to be coupled in performance. The sonatas that Scarlatti grouped this way were always related, as Kirkpatrick put it, by "contrast or complement," frequently in the major and minor modes of the same key (such as C major and C minor) or in the relative major and minor (such as C major and A minor).

Most of the sonatas are made up of two approximately equal parts, both of which are repeated. The first part starts in the home key, but modulates to another key. The second part begins in the foreign tonality and, by modulation, ends up back in the original key. Some sonatas contain but one single theme; others are made up of several separate motifs.

The Scarlatti sonatas can be identified in one of two ways: Either the Longo number (L), based on a catalog prepared in 1913 by Alessandro Longo, or the Kirkpatrick number (K), which comes from Ralph Kirkpatrick's more accurate 1953 listing.

Because Scarlatti wrote most of the sonatas while in Spain,

many are pervaded by that country's musical style. The **Sonata in C, K. 159 (L. 104)**, among the most popular, has the rhythms of a *jota,* a popular Spanish dance. Others with the same flavor are the **Sonata in G, K. 5 (L. 290)**, **Sonata in D, K. 387 (L. 14)**, and **Sonata in F, K. 468 (L. 279)**. Some, such as the **Sonata in D, K. 96 (L. 465)**, present the characteristic repeated note of flamenco music. Several imitate the strumming of a Spanish guitar; a few with this particular effect are the **Sonata in B flat, K. 249 (L. 39)**, **Sonata in C, K. 309 (L. 454)**, and **Sonata in E minor, K. 394 (L. 275)**.

One of the best-known Scarlatti sonatas, the **Sonata in G minor, K. 30 (L. 499)**, "**Cat Fugue**," is truly a fugue with particularly wide, almost irrational leaps (Kirkpatrick called them "bizarre intervals") between the notes. The melody led some imaginative commentator to decide that the composer took his inspiration from a cat strolling across the harpsichord keyboard, stepping on the melody notes—despite the complete lack of any supporting evidence.

Franz Schubert

Born January 31, 1797, in Vienna
Died November 19, 1828, in Vienna

SCHUBERT, perhaps the greatest song composer of all time, turned out some six hundred lieder of incredible beauty in his brief thirty-one years of life. The exceedingly large number of songs underscores Schubert's very special predilection for melody and the essentially lyrical approach he used. Every note he wrote, no matter whether for solo instrument, chamber group, or full orchestra, conveys a strongly vocal, in contrast with a typically instrumental, quality. Even the thematic material from which Schubert fashions his instrumental music tends to take the form of prolonged, songlike melodic lines, rather than the terse motifs that provide the basis of works by such composers as Beethoven and Haydn.

From the absence of concertos in his oeuvre we can gather that virtuosity for its own sake was alien to Schubert's musical thinking. From his biography we also know that few sonatas were intended for specific performers or performances or to fulfill commissions from publishers, since during his lifetime there was virtually no interest in his music outside a small circle of friends and admirers. One can safely assume, therefore, that the main reason Schubert created music was self-expression and that, fortunately for us, his inspiration led him to write many sonatas.

Few of Schubert's compositions were performed or published during his lifetime, making it extremely difficult to arrange his music in chronological order. The task was finally accomplished by Otto Deutsch, an Austrian musicologist, who published a thematic catalog that appeared in English translation in 1951. The only reliable ordering of Schubert's music, therefore, is by D (Deutsch) number. The opus numbers offer no help at all; as one egregious example, an early piano sonata from 1817 is Op. 164, while his last sonata, composed in 1826, is Op. 78.

The **Sonata for Arpeggione and Piano, D. 821,** was composed in November 1824 and is the sole sonata that was commissioned of Schubert. It is also the only surviving major work for the arpeggione. This instrument, invented in 1823 by Georg Stauffer, was a cross between a cello (because it was held between the knees and bowed) and a guitar (because it was fretted and had six strings). The arpeggione's leading promoter was performer Vincenz Schuster, who asked Schubert to write the sonata and then gave the premiere performance. Since the arpeggione never gained wide acceptance and soon disappeared completely, Schubert's publisher had the prescience to print the music with alternative parts for cello or violin replacing the arpeggione; later editions also include a viola part.

Although some critics dismiss the "Arpeggione," as the sonata is universally known, as a lesser work, it is a popular repertoire piece, particularly for cellists and violists, and an audience favorite. Cast in three movements, the first charms with its glorious outpouring of melody and maintains its good humor in spite of the minor key. The short second movement continues even more songlike, while the finale, which follows without pause, exudes its own special gaiety and exuberance.

Piano Sonatas

Between the years 1815 and 1828 Schubert composed more than twenty piano sonatas. The number is vague because some sonatas were not so entitled and some were left incomplete. Just as it was not death that prevented Schubert from finishing the "Unfinished" Symphony, so one distraction or another made him turn his attention to other compositions and leave several of the sonatas in their incomplete state.

The earliest sonata to be firmly established in the current repertoire is the **Piano Sonata in A, D. 664 (Op. 120),** which

Schubert probably composed in July 1819, age twenty-two, while spending a summer holiday at Steyr in Upper Austria. His host was iron merchant Josef von Köller, and the young composer dedicated the gentle, appealing sonata to Köller's "very pretty" eighteen-year-old daughter, Josephine. The sonata may have been offered to the young woman as a token of Schubert's affection at the time, but there is some evidence that he subsequently asked her to return the manuscript.

The "Little A major," sonata as it is called (to avoid confusion with the later and larger D. 959 in the same key), is a comparatively short piece that projects a pleasant warmth and geniality. Its delightful tunefulness has made it a repertoire staple.

The limpid and ingratiating opening theme of the first movement precedes a more rhythmic subsidiary theme. The climax of the movement comes in the development section, after which Schubert restates both themes and ends with a coda. The simple Andante, in three-part song form (ABA), maintains the initial rhythmic pattern throughout. To add to the good humor of the sprightly last movement, Schubert occasionally breaks in with a catchy waltzlike tune.

Composed nearly four years later, in February 1823, the **Piano Sonata in A minor, D. 784 (Op. 143)**, offers quite a contrast to the "Little A major" sonata. Instead of being inviting, it is rather distant; instead of mostly speaking in soft, dulcet tones, it alternately shouts and whispers; and instead of being intimate in scale it is large and spacious. In it Schubert replaces the open-faced, ingenuous air of the "Little A major" sonata with a secretive and slightly mysterious quality.

This somewhat bleak and stark sonata begins with an evocative theme that seems overlaid with meaning as it trudges on with its marchlike cadence, quickly rising to a forceful peroration. A meltingly beautiful second theme acts as a foil to the foreboding opening. Much use of unison and of trills and tremolo characterize the entire movement, with occasional explosive outbursts that interrupt the flow of the music.

The principal theme of the Andante, a broad, arching melody, has a puzzling little rhythmic figure at the end of each phrase. Schubert then uses the rhythmic figure as the transition to the agitated middle section and ends with a free repetition of the opening.

Three musical gestures inform the entire last movement: First, a scurrying passage of rapid notes that turns on itself in a sort of curling motion; second, a powerful staccato rhythmic pattern that sends out jets of flashing scales; and third, a lovely, tender lyrical melody. Using these three ideas as the structural elements, Schubert welds together an exciting, dramatic movement.

During just one year, 1825, Schubert created three of his finest piano sonatas—D. 840, 845, and 850. Of them, the first might well have achieved recognition as one of his greatest sonatas—but unfortunately he left it unfinished. The second, the **Piano Sonata in A minor, D. 845 (Op. 42)**, also an outstanding work, regrettably is seldom played, possibly because its extreme length—it lasts more than thirty minutes—offers some programming problems.

A strangely melancholy air hangs over the moderate-tempo opening movement of this sonata. An overall spirit of resignation pervades; even the strong, energetic sections do not seem capable of breaking through the extensive gloom.

The second movement, a theme and variations, offers a particularly telling example of Schubert's lyrical, cantabile style. A letter that mentions this movement, written on July 25, 1825, to his parents, furnishes further evidence of the great importance he attached to the vocal quality of his music, both in the writing and in the playing: "What pleased especially were the variations in my new Sonata for two hands, which I performed alone and not without merit, since several people assured me that the keys became singing voices under my hands, which, if true, pleases me greatly, since I cannot endure the accursed chopping in which even distinguished piano players indulge and which delights neither the ear nor the mind." In this movement, Schubert puts a direct, straightforward theme through five variations, none of them going far from the original melody. The first two variations are essentially preparatory for the highly emotional and impassioned third variation. The intensity stays high for the next variation, but there is an air of relaxation and tranquillity about the fifth and final reworking of the theme. A brief coda ends the movement.

The clear, fanfarelike Scherzo clears the air after the seriousness of the Andante. A gently rocking middle section is heard before the return of the scherzo section.

Possessed of great internal energy, the finale surges forward, now with brilliant rapid passagework, now with striking question-and-answer phrases, until it reaches the powerful ending.

Schubert composed the last of the 1825 sonatas, the **Piano Sonata in D, D. 850 (Op. 53)**, in just three weeks during that summer. Very likely, the fact that it was dedicated to Karl Maria von Bocklet, a professional pianist, enabled Schubert to include a number of technically difficult effects. Schubert's great admirer, composer Robert Schumann, provided this brief description of the work: "What a different kind of life wells up from the energetic D major sonata, seizing us and sweeping us away, stroke upon stroke! Then the adagio, wholly Schubertian, impulsive, extravagant, scarcely can he find an ending. The last movement is difficult to fit into the whole and is rather comic. To consider it from a serious viewpoint would be utterly ridiculous."

When Schubert's publisher issued what we now call the **Piano Sonata in G, D. 894 (Op. 78)**, he offered it as four separate piano pieces—Fantasia, Andante, Menuetto, and Allegretto—in the hope, one guesses, of increasing sales. But there can be little question that Schubert conceived it as a sonata. And a fine one it is, leading Robert Schumann to call it "the most perfect of his sonatas in form and spirit."

Completed in October 1826, the G major sonata starts with a movement in moderate tempo. The first theme seems strangely arcane, while the more animated second subject is enlivened with snatches of waltz melody. The tension and intensity mount in the development, and the remainder of the movement concerns itself with a restatement of the two themes and a short coda.

The affectionate quality of the Andante's main theme, despite its somewhat homely, slightly awkward quality, manages to insinuate itself into the listener's memory. The subsidiary subject, which begins as a blustery affair, grows more subdued after the original onslaught. The entire movement is essentially a rather free alternation of these two ideas.

The delightful Menuetto was much favored during Schubert's lifetime, and modern audiences are equally beguiled by the charms of this irresistible miniature.

Some performers mistakenly tend to make the finale a dazzling, high-speed display piece. But those who follow Schubert's tempo indication of Allegretto ("Somewhat fast") give the main theme a rustic, naive air and an appeal that is far more consonant with the composer's intention. Various passages that hint at perpetual motion are heard between the appearances of the prime subject but it is the main theme, with its repeated-note ending, that dominates the movement.

In September 1828, at age thirty-one, Schubert found himself at a particularly low ebb. A chronic illness had caused all his hair to fall out, a condition that he hid by wearing a wig. He could find neither performers to play his music nor publishers to print it, and, perhaps most disappointing of all to him, no opera house was interested in producing his operas, written or projected. Always a poor businessman, he had earned virtually nothing from the few successes he had scored and was hard pressed to support himself. And to compound matters, the large group of friends that had always surrounded him was dwindling and he was desperately lonely.

Nonetheless, it was under these particularly difficult and trying circumstances that Schubert wrote his glorious last three sonatas during a period of just three weeks ending on September 26, 1828. On September 27, Schubert achieved a final triumph as he played the pieces to the acclaim of his small social circle. Thereafter his health deteriorated quickly, leading to his death on November 19.

The **Piano Sonata in C minor, D. 958,** is probably the least popular of Schubert's last three sonatas. One can only speculate on a couple of possibilities: Is it due to the sonata's overall somber mien? Or because the themes themselves are not especially distinctive or arresting? No matter the reason, it surely is a sonata worthy of more frequent performance.

Although the tempo marking of the first movement is Allegro ("Fast"), in a preliminary sketch Schubert marked it Allegro moderato ("Moderately fast"), perhaps to indicate that it should be played somewhat more slowly than a full-speed Allegro. While the terse opening statement invites comparison with Beethoven, the highly eloquent development section more clearly expresses Schubert's individuality. The movement's whispered ending is a truly inspired touch.

The songlike slow movement alternates two basic musical ideas—the first solemn and leisurely, the second broad and spacious.

Almost shy and reticent, the short minuet that follows presents a subdued, wistful countenance. Although the piano writing has moments of brilliance, the overwhelming impression is one of great delicacy.

Enormous in size, the rondo finale takes the listener on a far-flung musical journey. Galloping bravely along, the movement tries to introduce a bit of good cheer into the proceedings, but never completely succeeds in lightening the prevailing mood.

The **Piano Sonata in A, D. 959,** starts with a grand, majestic statement of the opening theme. But the magisterial effect is soon eclipsed by the simple, charming subsidiary subject. And Schubert, recognizing the tender beauty of the second theme, makes it the dominant idea of the entire movement.

As in the preceding sonata, the slow movement is a song, a plaintive lament, transferred to the piano. The movement gets some of its special dramatic intensity from the use of recitative—metrically free writing in imitation of speech.

Airy and gay in character, the scherzo resembles a light-hearted interlude. With a little imagination one can easily hear some string pizzicato notes in the piano writing.

The concluding rondo surely ranks among Schubert's best; it supplies a most fitting cap to a truly outstanding sonata.

Few challenge the supremacy of the **Piano Sonata in B flat, D. 960,** Schubert's last effort in the form. Of all his piano sonatas, this contemplative and deeply felt work is also most frequently performed and recorded.

The first movement, one of the longest and quietest in all the sonatas, abounds with a generous amount of thematic material. Phrase after phrase of beautiful melody pours forth, communicating both gentle yearning and peaceful resignation. A low trill, which is heard a few times, gives the movement a cryptic air of mystery and foreboding.

In an audacious stroke, Schubert places two rather slow movements in succession, following the Molto moderato ("Very moderate") first movement with an Andante sostenuto ("Slow and sustained") second movement. But it works. Some hear in the highly emotional Andante sostenuto a consoling expression of affirmation; others quite differently find it a heart-piercing paradigm of pain and pathos. No matter how it is perceived, few fail to be touched by this highly affecting music.

The Scherzo—gay, sparkling, and light of foot—offers a welcome contrast to the slow solemnity of the first two movements. The middle part, the Trio, introduces a more sober, if not ominous, note. But the return of the Scherzo ends the movement in the same high spirited way as it began.

Although slightly slower than the Scherzo, the finale sets out with even more splendor and joy. The carefree and jaunty principal subject resembles the type of simple tune that one sings in the shower or whistles on a stroll. The subsidiary theme is heard twice, its highly melodramatic quality impinging on the main theme's brightness. But the good feelings prevail—and there results a truly happy, if not exultant, ending.

Violin Sonatas

Schubert was plagued with various kinds of difficulties throughout the year 1816. After having taught for two years in a position he detested, he had applied for the post of music director of a school in Laibach, and had been rejected. He wanted to marry the singer Therese Grob, but could not afford to support a wife. And even though he was turning out page after page of incredible music, everything from songs to sonatas to symphonies, virtually none of his works were being performed or published.

Nevertheless, during March and April of that year Schubert wrote a set of three sonatas for violin and piano—tight, compact works that are technically undemanding for either violinist or pianist. Schubert originally entitled them Sonatas for Piano with Violin Accompaniment. But when they were finally printed some twenty years later, the publisher called them Sonatinas, thereby implying that they were "easy" pieces suitable for students or amateurs. Although these particular violin sonatas are well within the grasp of most technically advanced students, they do require a high level of interpretative ability.

The **Violin Sonata in D, D. 384 (Op. 137, No. 1)**, strikes most listeners as bright, clear, and wonderfully agreeable. The melodic interest in the first movement centers on the opening theme. In the course of its first statement, Schubert presents the theme no fewer than three different ways—in a soft unison, in free imitation, and in a loud unison declaration.

Permeated with grace and elegance, the Andante takes a nostalgic look back at a more courtly era. After presenting the main theme in major, Schubert goes on to a slightly more active section in minor, and then brings back the original melody in the piano with the violin weaving a delicate tracery around it.

What a delightful, swaggering tune Schubert created for the final rondo! With occasional touches of sentimentality, the good humor bubbles through the entire movement.

The quiet opening of the **Violin Sonata in A minor, D. 385 (Op. 137, No. 2)**, does little to disguise the fact that the melody itself is made up of seemingly unrelated notes with immense, jolting leaps from one equally long note to the next, all moving deliberately over a pulsating accompaniment. The fiery, impassioned violin entrance, stretching the jumps over even greater distances, heightens the dramatic impact. But, in keeping with Schubert's concise approach, the raging fires are soon banked for a lovely, guileless second theme. After repeating the two themes, but with scarcely any development of either one, they are both brought back for a literal reprise, except for the adjustment of the keys, and a few concluding notes.

Schubert's great gift as a creator of song melody is heard to stunning effect in the Andante. First one instrument and then the other sings the several vocal melodies of this highly appealing, though somewhat poignant, movement.

The predominantly strong, loud, and forceful Menuetto, with its bold, incisive rhythms, could have been written by Beethoven. For contrast, the flowing middle section, the Trio, remains relatively quiet throughout, leading to a shortened review of the Menuetto that brings the movement to an end.

The finale offers little more than the alternation of two contrasting musical ideas. The first is a tranquil singing melody built up of a pithy phrase that is repeated several times sequentially; the other is an active, angry section, also founded on a short motif, which is essentially treated the same way.

The stark, startling opening phrase of the **Violin Sonata in G minor, D. 408 (Op. 137, No. 3)**, provides the generative force for the entire first movement. While most of the melodic material derives from its bold, slashing rhythm, the music quickly changes from the original gruff character to one of compliant sweetness.

Many consider the second movement a homage to Mozart. First the violin presents its eighteenth-century–sounding melody, and the piano responds with a tune of similar character. A more excited middle section precedes a somewhat decorated return of the opening two melodies.

The Menuetto switches back and forth between violent outbursts and quiet, delicate responses. The Trio in the middle has but one musical idea—a subdued, gently rocking melody in the violin over a flowing piano accompaniment, with some hints of imitation in the left hand. At the end the Menuetto is repeated.

Although moderate in speed, the last movement has a buoyant lilt that creates the impression, at times, of a Gypsy folk dance. Short in length, the movement builds to a loud, flashy conclusion.

The first three violin sonatas were published as Sonatinas, and the fourth, the **Violin Sonata in A, D. 574 (Op. 162)**, was published—fifteen years after its completion in 1817—as a Duo. Organized in the traditional four movements, the sonata consists of a first movement notable for its profusion of melodies, a high-speed second-movement scherzo, a slow movement with a sort of distant, subdued air about it, and a finale that bears a close kinship to the earlier Scherzo.

Robert Schumann

Born June 8, 1810, in Zwickau, Germany
Died July 29, 1856, in Endenich, Germany

ROBERT SCHUMANN, considered by many to be the true voice
of Romanticism, once stated his artistic credo: "To send light
into the depths of the human heart." So impassioned, emotional,
and subjective are his sonatas, for example, that they can well be
classified as tone poems for one or two instruments. Yet, despite
the primacy of feeling and expression in every note he wrote,
Schumann was always aware of the traditions and styles that he
inherited from the past Classical era, and used them as the bed-
rock for his highly romantic compositions.

Of all Schumann's sonatas—three for piano and two for violin
and piano—the **Piano Sonata No. 1 in F-sharp minor, Op. 11,**
can best be cited as the *echt* Romantic sonata. Even the mysterious title Schumann wrote on the music—"To Clara, from
Florestan and Eusebius," without any further identification of
the composer—contributed to the work's Romantic aura. It was
only Schumann's closest friends who knew that Florestan and
Eusebius were two characters created in the composer's imagination to represent the opposing sides of his personality—
Florestan, the passionate, action-oriented, idealistic slayer of Phi-
listines, and Eusebius, reflective, introspective, deliberate, and
traditional. Not until the second edition, published in 1840, was
Schumann openly acknowledged as the composer.

The First Piano Sonata, completed in 1835 when the composer was twenty-five years old, fervently declares young
Schumann's love for pianist and composer Clara Wieck, who was

to become his wife five years later, over the violent objections of her father. Schumann once described the work to Clara as a "unique cry of passion in which your theme appears in all possible forms."

Schumann used the words "your theme" literally. He expressed his passion with a melody that he borrowed from one of Clara's own musical compositions, *Scène fantastique.* Both the accompaniment to the main subject of the first movement and the lyrical second theme were based on this melody. The principal theme of the movement, though, Schumann derived from his own piano piece *Fandango,* which he had composed in 1831. This powerful, expressive initial movement follows a slow introduction whose melody comes from a Schumann song, "To Anna" (1828).

The principal subject of the second movement, entitled Aria, is the same "To Anna" theme. Perhaps Liszt described Aria best when he called it "one of the most beautiful pages we know . . . a song of great passion, expressed with a fullness and calm."

The Florestan side of Schumann's nature dominates the fast-tempo third and fourth movements. Exuberant in spirit, they place exceptional virtuosic demands on the performer.

The **Piano Sonata No. 2 in G minor, Op. 22,** the most popular and best liked of the three, also underwent the longest period of gestation. Schumann composed the first and third movements in 1833; the second movement began as a song, "Im Herbst," in 1828 and became a piano piece, "Andantino," two years later, before he reworked it into its final form for the sonata. Schumann composed the finale in 1838, but when Clara declared it "much too difficult," he wrote a new concluding movement. (The original finale is published as a separate piano piece, "Presto Passionato.")

The opening movement of the G minor sonata proceeds in a fiery, intense, and very pianistic manner. Its clear organization progresses from the stormy first theme, through the poetic second theme, to the working out of both themes in the development section, and ends with their return in the recapitulation. (In addition to its stirring musical qualities, the movement is noted for its paradoxical tempo indications: marked to be played "As fast as possible" at the beginning, the music carries the instruction near the end for the performer to play "Faster," and "Still faster" at the very close!)

Schumann, quite obviously, was thinking in vocal terms when he composed the second movement, which he structured as a warm, songlike melody over a simple accompaniment. As for the style, the music seems to have been created under the sway of the gentle, dreamy Eusebius side of Schumann's musical personality.

Vigorous and vital in character, the third movement immediately and abruptly changes the mood from pensive reflection to rambunctious good fun.

Schumann based the main theme of the finale on an earlier piano piece, *Papillons*. Cast in rondo form, the movement conveys an extremely sectional feeling due to striking differences of tempo and mood between the primary subject and the contrasting interludes.

The **Piano Sonata No. 3 in F minor, Op. 14,** began life in 1835 and 1836 as a five-movement piece for solo piano that Schumann simply entitled Concerto. At the publisher's request, however, the composer dropped the two scherzo movements and changed the name to Concerto Without Orchestra. Published in that form as Op. 14, Schumann put the work through further revisions, making minor changes in the outer movements, restoring a scherzo as the second movement, and cutting two of the six variations in the third. Despite the fact that the third sonata has a lower opus number than the second sonata, Number 3 was actually completed after Number 2.

Central to the entire F minor sonata is a descending melodic line known as "Andantino de Clara Wieck," taken from an original piece composed by Clara. This line, or theme, is heard in some form in every movement. The musical focus of the sonata is the slow movement, a theme and variations, based directly on Clara's theme. Brahms gave the premiere in Vienna in 1862, but the sonata never found much favor with pianists and today is rarely performed.

Schumann tended to write clusters of similar works at one

time. Until 1839, he essentially just wrote piano music; 1840 was devoted to songs; in 1841 symphonies took his fancy; and his chamber music all came after 1842—including the two violin sonatas, the **Violin Sonata No. 1 in A minor, Op. 105,** and **Violin Sonata No. 2 in D minor, Op. 121.** Composed in the early 1850s, shortly before his 1854 hospitalization with what is now believed to have been a manic-depressive disorder, these two sonatas are only occasionally encountered on recital programs. Schumann's creative spark produced some very fine music in both these works for violin, on a level equal to his most outstanding compositions, despite some feeling that his worsening mental illness robbed them of their full realization. In point of fact, the writing is neither grateful nor idiomatic for the two instruments and the persistence of the minor mode in both sonatas makes them sound overly somber and fatalistic.

Alexander Scriabin

Born January 6, 1872, in Moscow
Died April 17, 1915, in Moscow

I am God!
I am nothing, I am play, I am freedom, I am life.
I am the boundary, I am the peak.

So wrote Alexander Scriabin, surely one of the most original, imaginative, and visionary of all composers. To Scriabin, creating music was not just a matter of placing notes on a five-line staff—it was a mystical, spiritual act of faith that sprang, unbidden, from his innermost being. "The external world is the result of my subjective spiritual activity," he said. At another time he stated his credo: "Art must unite with philosophy and religion in an indivisible whole to form a new Gospel that will replace the old Gospel, which we have outlived. I cherish the dream of creating such a 'Mystery.' " Scriabin devoted his entire creative life with great singleness of purpose to the end of discovering the way to express this "mystery" in music.

Upon graduation from the Moscow Conservatory in 1892, Scriabin began teaching there, as well as performing and touring as piano virtuoso. Around that same time, he composed a number of piano works, including the **Piano Sonata No. 1 in F, Op. 6; Piano Sonata No. 2 in G-sharp minor, Op. 19, "Fantasy Sonata"; Piano Sonata No. 3 in F-sharp minor, Op. 23, "State of Soul"; and Piano Sonata No. 4 in F sharp, Op. 30**—pieces that drew much of their inspiration from the earlier Romantic piano compositions of Chopin and Liszt.

When compared to the two earliest sonatas, the third marks a distinct departure from the musical path on which Scriabin had embarked. The subtitle, "State of Soul," refers to the programmatic, or extramusical, content of the music. The composer describes the four parts, which correspond to the movements of the music: the soul cast into a sea of strife, the soul floundering, the illusion and transience of rest, and the ecstasy of the struggle.

Scriabin moved even further from his original youthful style in the popular Fourth Sonata. He announces the timid, tentative principal theme at the outset, and then, throughout the one-movement sonata, imbues the melody with ever increasing strength and assurance until the end, when he presents it in a powerful, grandiose peroration. This scheme clearly expresses the program of the music, which the composer describes as the transformation of a dimly seen distant blue star into a blazing yellow sun.

In 1903, with the announcement "I can't bear to hear other people's music all day long and then write my own at night," Scriabin gave up teaching and playing to devote all of his energies to composition and the realization of his unique musical vision.

The **Piano Sonata No. 5 in F sharp, Op. 53,** of 1908 takes on even more of the aura of the occult than Scriabin's earlier compositions. Musically he makes considerable use of his so-called mystic chord. While traditional harmony uses chords consisting of notes a third apart, the notes of the mystic chord are separated by intervals of a fourth. Scriabin constructed the chord from the high overtones, overtones 9, 10, 11, 13, and 14, of the fundamental note C. (Overtones are higher-pitched notes present, but unheard, in every musical sound; they give the sound its particular tone color, making it possible, for instance, to tell the difference between a flute and a violin playing the exact same note.) The notes of the mystic chord are C, F-sharp, B-flat, E, A, and D.

Programmatically, Scriabin inscribed this brief original poem on the manuscript of his Fifth Sonata:

I call you to life, O forces of mystery!
Submerged in obscure depths.
O thou creative spirit, fearful of life,
I bring to you my courage!

Scriabin's embrace of the supernatural grows even stronger in the **Piano Sonata No. 6 in G, Op. 62,** of 1911, a more subdued work with a striking, hushed, mysterious opening, and the **Piano Sonata No. 7 in F sharp, Op. 6, "The White Mass,"** of 1912, the composer's favorite, with its harsh dissonances and its particularly wild, frenetic dance-like ending.

The year 1913 saw the composition of Scriabin's last three sonatas. The **Piano Sonata No. 8 in A, Op. 66,** the longest work in this form, has not engendered much favor or interest among modern performers. With the **Piano Sonata No. 9 in F, Op. 68, "The Black Mass,"** Scriabin moves to an even deeper mystical level. The composer left no clues to the meaning of his subtitle beyond the accepted definition of a black Mass as a satanic rite or ritual. That it is an appropriate name becomes clear as one listens to the music, in which passages of deeply felt religious fervor alternate with sections of demonic rage, and moments of frenzied abandon overwhelm parts of beatific serenity. Traditional harmony, melody, and form all become subservient to the central cause, which is to express in sound Scriabin's religious-philosophical-musical visions.

The **Piano Sonata No. 10 in C, Op. 70,** ranks high among Scriabin's most performed scores, despite the fact that its meaning and musical message are particularly obscure and elusive. Scriabin's comment: "My Tenth Sonata is a sonata of insects. Insects are born from the sun, they are the sun's kisses. How unified world-understanding is when you look at things this way." But beyond the rather naive buzzing and whirring insect-like sounds that Scriabin calls forth from the piano, a musical message of strong emotions and great beauty emerges.

Dmitri Shostakovich

Born September 25, 1906, in St. Petersburg
Died August 9, 1975, in Moscow

NOW universally acknowledged to be a major voice of twentieth-century music, during his lifetime Shostakovich had a check-
ered career at home, falling in and out of favor with Communist
party officials. After the huge success of his First Symphony in
1926, his satirical opera *The Nose* (1930) was soundly de-
nounced as "bourgeois decadence" and criticized for lacking the
all-important "social realism." Shostakovich returned to favor
with his First Piano Concerto in 1933, but received an even
worse drubbing for his opera *Lady Macbeth of Mtsensk;* the denun-
ciation appeared in *Pravda* on January 28, 1936, under the head-
line MUDDLE INSTEAD OF MUSIC.

Each of his works over the following years was received with
reactions that varied from enthusiastic approval to angry scold-
ing, until the famous attack by the Central Committee of the
Communist party on February 10, 1948, when Shostakovich—
and Prokofiev—were accused of "formalist perversions and an-
tidemocratic tendencies in music." (Interestingly enough, there
is no clear definition of "formalist perversions"; one does note,
however, that it is widely used by Soviet officials to describe
almost all experimental or avant-garde compositions.)

As a consequence of the political-musical situation in the Soviet Union, Shostakovich composed two distinctly different
kinds of music: public music, including the major orchestral and
stage works, which sought to meet the perceived needs of the
Soviet state; and private music, including the sonatas and other

chamber music, in which he felt free to express his innermost thoughts and feelings, without concern for the obligatory conformity to state standards.

Soon after graduating from the Leningrad Conservatory in 1926 Shostakovich composed his **Piano Sonata No. 1, Op. 12.** Four major influences shaped the music: the pressure from the powerful RAPM (Russian Association of Proletarian Musicians) to produce compositions that served to advance the Soviet revolution; the traditional compositional practices he was taught in school; the new directions taken by such composers as Stravinsky, Prokofiev, and Hindemith; and finally his need to be true to his creative instincts and to develop a unique and original voice. The massive, one-movement First Sonata makes strenuous virtuosic technical demands on the performer, with its many percussive effects and passages of harsh dissonance. Yet stylistically the work owes a considerable debt to traditional Western models, resulting in a simplicity and formal clarity that give the piece an overall Neoclassical character.

Despite the vitriolic attack on Shostakovich following a performance of *Lady Macbeth of Mtsensk* in Moscow in 1936, the opera had premiered with great success two years earlier in Leningrad. And it was in the afterglow of the earlier triumph that Shostakovich wrote the **Sonata for Cello and Piano, Op.** 40—a serious, profound, and intensely personal composition.

The introspective first movement revolves around two themes: a broad, elegiac melody that builds to a fervid climax before subsiding to a much more romantic and emotional tune. The basic rhythmic pattern of the Moderato con moto resembles a waltz that Shostakovich enlivens with added touches of wit, humor, and satire. The somber, severe, and very slow third movement, a tragic song of sorrow, serves as the sonata's gravitational center. Shostakovich lightens matters with the last movement, which scintillates with high-spirited good cheer; the joyfulness is enhanced by touches of jazz and a glorious soaring melody near the middle.

In 1942, soon after learning of the death of Leonid Nikolayev, his piano teacher at the conservatory, Shostakovich began the **Piano Sonata No. 2, Op. 61,** which he dedicated to the memory of his mentor and completed the following year. One device he employed in the composition was to take mundane or even trivial melodies and treat them in a serious manner. This gave the piece a certain ambiguity: if one focuses on the themes, the music sounds cheerful; if one focuses on the treatment, it sounds mournful. The sonata opens with a fast, energetic movement, making for a strong, resolute beginning. In sharp contrast, the Largo sounds fragile and delicate, an evocative example of night music. Since Nikolayev particularly enjoyed variation form, Shostakovich ends the tribute sonata with a theme and eleven variations. The composer's affection comes through very clearly here, as he puts the simple, straightforward theme through its heartfelt, emotional variations, none of which depart very far from the original.

Composed for violinist David Oistrakh's sixtieth birthday in 1968, the big-scaled **Sonata for Violin and Piano, Op. 134,** assumes an approach that is at once stark and uncompromising. An experimental composition, it begins with a striding theme in the piano, ascending and descending, that proves to be a twelve-tone row and its inversion. The row is based on Arnold Schoenberg's "method of composing with twelve notes," which in effect held that all the notes of the chromatic scale must be heard before any can be repeated. This twelve-tone method becomes a tightly-structured way of composing that deliberately and purposefully avoids any feeling of key or tonality. While Schoenberg rigorously confined his twelve-tone compositions to various manipulations of the tone row, Shostakovich used the row more freely as a traditional theme, and fashioned the movement out of its development and varied repeats.

The second movement, a scherzo, sounds uncharacteristically brusque and vigorous, with much heavy pounding in the piano and strong accents in the violin.

Contrary to usual practices, the tempo of the last movement is slow; the short Largo introduction leads to the slightly faster Andante body of the movement, where the violin states the theme in dry, simple pizzicato (plucked) notes. With a keen ear for instrumental effects and sonorities, Shostakovich repeats the theme over and over again in ever shifting tonal settings and variations, bringing it up to an overwhelming climax before letting it grow quiet and fade away.

Shostakovich's last sonata, and final composition, is his **Sonata for Viola and Piano, Op.** 147, which he completed on July 5, 1975, just one month before his death. Like his String Quartet No. 15, this sonata seemingly deals with the thoughts and feelings the seriously ill composer had about his impending demise. Sublime and serene, the work takes a penetrating look into the abyss of death and reacts with composure and acceptance, rather than fear, anger, or despair.

The dramatic, yet intimate, first movement, which Shostakovich described as being "like a novella," has the two instruments conversing and interacting throughout—the only exception being the brief viola monologue near the end. This movement, and the two that follow, conclude quietly, with Shostakovich's direction *morendo* ("dying") written on the music.

The second movement, although not so marked, is a scherzo, with a smooth, sinuous middle section that comes between the sprightly, playful opening and closing parts. In spite of the gay, carefree surface impression, one detects an underlying tension and anxiety.

Shostakovich dedicated the slow last movement "to the memory of a great composer, Beethoven." After an unaccompanied introduction by the viola, both instruments state the principal theme, an obvious derivation from Beethoven's "Moonlight" Sonata. The highly emotional, poignant movement reaches an impassioned climax after the viola cadenza, and then the music grows hushed and quiet allowing the two instruments to disappear in the final *morendo*.

Richard Strauss

Born June 11, 1864, in Munich
Died September 8, 1949, in Garmisch-Partenkirchen

DURING Strauss's growing-up years, composers such as Berlioz, Liszt, and especially Wagner were revolutionizing music, overthrowing many of the long-accepted canons of traditional composition and vastly expanding the vocabulary and range of music. But Richard's father, Franz Strauss, the leading French-horn player in Munich, would have none of this "modern" music. In the elder Strauss's view, few of the new compositions could compare with the works of such venerable nineteenth-century masters as Mendelssohn, Brahms, and Schumann.

It is only natural therefore, that young Richard—who showed his musical talent at an early age, playing piano at four, adding violin shortly thereafter, and composing at six—would show the influence of his father's musical heroes in his first published works. Since his only sonatas—for piano, cello and piano, and violin and piano—were written from 1880 to 1888, when Richard was between ages sixteen and twenty-four, all tended to follow the accepted, somewhat conservative tradition his father favored.

The strong impact of Mendelssohn's *Misdummer Night's Dream, Phantasie,* Op. 28, and *Capriccio brillant* can be detected in the earliest sonata Strauss wrote, the **Piano Sonata in B minor, Op. 5.** And, curiously enough, the main theme of the first movement is rhythmically identical to the famous signal motto of Beethoven's Fifth Symphony.

The **Sonata for Cello and Piano in F, Op. 6,** which followed the piano sonata by an interval of two years, shows Strauss's considerable maturation over that period. Here the harmonies are more adventuresome, the melodies more lyrical, and the music more authoritative—hints of the highly expressive romanticism that would dominate his later music.

Most commentators consider the second movement, the Andante, ma non troppo, the highpoint of the sonata. In three-part form—principal subject, contrast, return of the opening—the Andante is especially well written for the cello. While elements of the short, sentimental salon pieces that were so popular in the later nineteenth century are heard from time to time, the movement is immensely successful in bringing out the instrument's richest, most opulent sonorities. Other points worthy of mention are the fughetto that comes at the end of the first movement's development section and the *Till Eulenspiegel*-like third movement, which offers a foretaste of the tone poem Strauss composed a dozen years later.

With little question, the **Sonata for Violin and Piano in E flat, Op. 18,** composed in 1887 and 1888, ranks highest among the Strauss sonatas and shows the composer in complete control of the medium. Very thickly written parts, with many interweaving melodic lines, contribute to a density of texture that heralds Strauss's characteristically impressive orchestral works and operas.

The opening subject, first stated by the piano, sounds noble and resplendent, despite its underlying nervous energy. A broad, arching theme serves as the contrast. After a lengthy development section and a truncated recapitulation, the movement rises to an impassioned climax in the coda.

The Improvisation that follows (no one is quite sure why it is so named) was so popular that the publisher put it out as a separate violin piece. Sounding much like a Mendelssohn *Song Without Words,* the opening section soars songful and lyrical, the middle rings with intensity and passion, and the opening returns to conclude the symmetrical three-part movement.

In the final movement, Strauss almost seems to be trying to compress an entire orchestra into just two instruments. A short, slow piano introduction leads into the main theme of the fast body of the movement that sings out in full glory, bringing to mind one of the inspired melodies in Strauss's autobiographical tone poem *Ein Heldenleben.*

Although he was to live to age eighty-five, Strauss wrote no more sonatas after the violin sonata, which he composed when he was only twenty-four years old. Scholars have found an explanation in a letter Strauss wrote on August 24, 1888: "I have found myself in a gradually ever increasing contradiction between the musical-poetic content that I want to convey and the ternary sonata-form that has come down to us from the classical composers. This is only possible through a program."

Traditionally abstract works, sonatas bear little or no association with anything outside the music. And it was precisely this association, achieved by writing music with programmatic content, that interested Strauss and that he sought to incorporate in his compositions. Of course, he found the perfect medium for this expression not in sonatas, but in his well-known orchestral tone poems—among them *Don Juan, Death and Transfiguration, Also sprach Zarathustra,* and *Till Eulenspiegels lustige Streiche*—which occupied him, along with his operas, for the remaining six decades of his life.

Igor Stravinsky

Born June 17, 1882, in Oranienbaum, Russia
Died April 6, 1971, in New York City

THE year 1893 was a crucial one for the eleven-year-old Stravinsky. That was when he determined, despite his parents' opposition, to become a composer. And it was in October of that same year, at a performance at the Imperial Opera House in St. Petersburg, that Stravinsky caught a glimpse of his musical idol, Tchaikovsky. While the idea of a composing career formed early on, it took ten more years for Stravinsky to take the first steps toward realizing his goal by starting composition lessons with Nicolai Rimsky-Korsakov. Stravinsky's reverence for Tchaikovsky, however, can be seen in what he called his "first large-scale work," the **Piano Sonata (1904),** which evidences many characteristic devices of Tchaikovsky's musical style.

The sonata is exactly what one would expect from a twenty-one-year-old composer under the powerful influence of a titan like Tchaikovsky. While attracting listeners with its appealing melodies and rich romanticism, it also impresses with its scope and size, taking about a half hour to perform. Stravinsky dedicated the sonata to his friend Nicolas Richter, who performed it several times. But soon thereafter the score disappeared. Since Stravinsky had not kept a copy, and no one knew what had happened to the music Richter had used, the work remained unplayed for many years. In fact, as late as 1960, Stravinsky referred to the work as "the lost—fortunately lost—piano sonata."

Then, quite by accident, a copy was discovered in the Leningrad State Public Library in 1973, and after being published and recorded became an accepted part of the repertoire. Many enjoy the work for its many virtues as well as for the fascinating insights it offers into the musical thinking of the young Stravinsky.

In the years following the 1904 Piano Sonata, Stravinsky scandalized the musical world by producing his three famous ballets, *The Firebird, Petrouchka,* and *Le Sacre du printemps (The Rite of Spring).* To this day the frenzied rhythms, ferocious dissonances, primitivistic snatches of melody, and barely restrained barbarism make these works sound fresh and contemporary. Nevertheless, shortly after World War I, Stravinsky struck out in quite a different direction. He delineated his new course in an aphoristic dialogue. "Can a composer re-use the past and at the same time move in a forward direction?" he queried. And he answered, "Regardless of the answer (which is 'yes'), this academic question did not trouble me." In turning back to the past—to the music of such composers as Bach, Mozart, and Pergolesi—Stravinsky discovered a new source of inspiration. His own compositions in this style are usually referred to as Neoclassical, a term, incidentally, that Stravinsky scorned. The appellation persists, however, because it calls to mind the Classical roots of much of the music Stravinsky composed from about 1917 to 1927, which included such works as *Histoire du Soldat, Pulcinella,* and the Octet, as well as the Piano Sonata (1924).

Johann Sebastian Bach quite obviously inspired Stravinsky's 1924 Piano Sonata, which he wrote for his own use while launching his career as a piano soloist. But it was his own great skill and wit that shaped the final musical realization. The clear, crisp, and hard-edged writing strove, in Stravinsky's words, to achieve "terseness and lucidity."

The first movement captures the strong, energetic rhythmic drive of a fine Bach fast movement, carrying the music irresistibly forward from start to finish. The left-hand triplets continue without stop, played in unison by both hands for the first theme and accompanying a right-hand melody for the second. After stating the two themes, Stravinsky works them out and then brings them back, but in reverse order.

An arioso movement of a Bach cantata might well have served

as the model for the second-movement Adagietto. Here Stravinsky spins out a highly ornamented melody over a soft, staccato bass line—a pattern that brings to mind the sounds produced by an organist's feet lightly dancing over the pedals. The contrasting middle section replaces the marching bass with snappy two-note fillips before a return of the opening section.

"Bach's Two-Part Inventions were somewhere in the remote back of my mind while composing the last movement of the Piano Sonata," Stravinsky once explained. With rapid notes running throughout, Stravinsky combines the feeling of a Bach fugue with a more modern perpetual motion to craft a movement that is uniquely his own and an absolute delight to the ears.

Soon after the outbreak of World War II, Stravinsky came to the United States and settled in Hollywood, California. With the war, the composer's income from performances of his music dropped considerably and he accepted a number of commissions that he might not have taken in more normal times. Among these works are *Circus Polka,* a ballet for elephants, a fifteen-minute dance sequence *(Scènes de ballet)* for a Broadway musical, and *Ebony Concerto* for Woody Herman's dance band.

One piece he produced in 1944, though without a commission, was the **Sonata for Two Pianos.** Having chosen two pianos, "because four hands were needed to voice the linear contrapuntal style," he created a happy little work that reflects scarcely any of the pain and anguish he suffered as he learned of all the death and destruction caused by the continuing war.

The first movement, delightful and utterly captivating, has three melodic ideas—two tunes of naive, ingenuous charm separated by a slightly more agitated musical idea that is characterized by rapidly repeated notes. The three ideas are merely stated and repeated in slight variation before the disarming conclusion.

Simple and austere in melodic material and treatment, the following Theme and Variations is highly polyphonic, but with the various closely interconnected lines never obscuring the clarity of the writing. One variation includes a repeated-note figure that is slightly reminiscent of the first-movement theme.

The last movement recaptures the joyful character of the opening. Playful and rhythmically spicy, it starts with a bright saucy tune, which is briefly interrupted by a slightly more serious section and ends with the return of the original idea.

Like many other composers, Stravinsky was able to recall, often in detail, events surrounding the creation or performance of different works. The Two-Piano Sonata, he once confessed, reminded him of stuffed-up sinks. It seems that he was staying at the home of composer Darius Milhaud the only time he ever performed the sonata in public. Apparently Milhaud had been throwing coffee grounds into the sink for years, and it was while Stravinsky was there that the drainage pipes became completely blocked, requiring a major plumbing job to clear them out. And it was the stuffed pipes that the Two-Piano Sonata always evoked in Stravinsky's mind!

Antonio Vivaldi

Born March 4, 1676, in Venice
Died July 28, 1741, in Vienna

ALTHOUGH he was an ordained priest (called *il prete rosso,* "the red-haired priest," because of his hair color), Vivaldi said Mass for only a short period in 1703 due to a chronic chest ailment, now believed to be asthma. He subsequently took a position teaching music at the Ospedale della Pietà, a charitable institution for orphaned, illegitimate, and indigent girls, many of whom were extremely talented and received an excellent musical education. The word *ospedale* literally means hospital, but Pietà also came to be called a *conservatorio,* from which the English term conservatory, for music school, was derived.

Vivaldi spent a full thirty-six years at Pietà, with but a few interruptions. While there he turned out a huge quantity of music, mostly for his students, some of whom were outstanding performers who remained at the conservatory until they were middle-aged. Apart from his nearly four hundred concertos, Vivaldi composed sixty-one sonatas for a single instrument and harpsichord. Despite the fact that he created the sonatas while at Pietà, scholars believe that Vivaldi wrote them for private patrons, rather than for the students.

The period when Vivaldi was writing the sonatas—from about 1709 to 1740—marked a time of significant change in music. The older polyphonic texture, in which all the voices of a piece were treated independently and equally, was being replaced by the homophonic texture, with a single leading melodic line and a subservient accompaniment. Vivaldi managed to effect a synthesis of the two, sometimes using one texture, sometimes the other, and quite often slipping seamlessly back and forth within one composition.

The styles of the sonatas themselves were also sharply divided during this period. Some were church sonatas *(sonata da chiesa)*, which meant that they had the seriousness and abstract nature appropriate to church performance. The church sonatas usually started with a slow, solemn movement and included at least one fugue in a subsequent movement. The others were chamber sonatas *(sonata da camera)*. They were lighter in approach and consisted of a number of shorter pieces in different dance rhythms that were related in key or character. The first movement of a chamber sonata was usually a slow prelude, followed by the sequence of dances.

Just as he used both polyphony and homophony, so Vivaldi reconciled and combined the church and chamber sonata styles. Many of his church sonatas include dancelike movements, even if they are not so named. And a good number of his chamber sonatas are written with the polyphonic texture and weightiness of the sonata da chiesa.

All of Vivaldi's sonatas are for a solo instrument and *basso continuo,* which is also called figured bass or thoroughbass. In these works the composer furnishes a single bass line that guides the harpsichord player in deciding which chords and harmonies to build on the bass line. It also indicates that a low-sounding instrument, such as the cello, should play the bass line as well. In practice, most performances of the Vivaldi sonatas do not use the additional cello. The only exception is the Op. 2 violin sonatas, where the musical justification for using the cello stems from the great importance of the bass line and its many interactions with the violin part.

Although several scholars have prepared thematic catalogs of Vivaldi's music, the most reliable one was published in 1974 by the Danish musicologist Peter Ryom. His numbering system, which is used here, carries the identifying letters RV, standing for *Ryom Verzeichnis* ("Ryom Catalog").

Some scholars consider the nine **Sonatas for Cello and Harpsichord, RV. 38–41, 43–47,** Vivaldi's best chamber works. That he purportedly wrote some of his most deeply felt music for the lower-pitched instruments is evidenced by Vivaldi's forty bassoon concertos. In these nine sonatas, the composer seemingly delights in giving the cello a varied role—now singing out the melody, now supplying a bass underpinning to the harpsichord. Although structured like church sonatas, with the usual sequence of Slow, Fast, Slow, Fast movements, the actual mood and writing style inclines toward the chamber sonata. Six of the cello sonatas were published in 1740 and designated Op. 14. The others are individual compositions that are not further identified.

Vivaldi's forty violin sonatas belong in four groups. The earliest are the **Twelve Sonatas for Violin and Harpsichord, Op. 2, RV.** 1, 8, 9, 14, 16, 20, 21, 23, 27, 31, 32, 36, published in 1709. The individual movements bear the titles of dances, as found in chamber sonatas, but the titles also include tempo designations, which suggest church sonatas.

The **Four Sonatas for Violin and Harpsichord, Op. 5, RV.** 18, 30, 33, 35, were issued in 1716. In chamber style, each one begins with a Preludio, followed by a number of dances. The dances, however, are so far in style from the original dances that they create an unmistakable impression of church sonatas.

The remaining **24 Sonatas for Violin and Harpsichord, RV.** 2, 3, 5, 6, 10, 12, 13, 15, 16, 17a, 19, 22, 24–26, 28, 29, 34, and 755–760, also share attributes of both chamber and church sonatas.

In addition to the violin and cello sonatas, Vivaldi wrote six wind sonatas—**Four Sonatas for Flute, RV.** 48–51, **Sonata for Recorder, RV. 52,** and **Sonata for Oboe, RV. 53.**

A strange addendum to the list of Vivaldi sonatas is the set of **Six Sonatas for Musette (bagpipe), Vielle (hurdy-gurdy), Flute, Oboe, or Violin, Op. 13, RV. 54–59,** "Il pastor fido" ("The Faithful Shepherd"). Although often presented as an original composition by Vivaldi, *Il pastor fido* actually represents a spurious pastiche, put together by a French publisher from various works by Vivaldi and other composers.

Glossary

Baroque. The period in music from about 1600 to 1750 characterized by much use of decoration and ornamentation and a texture that tended toward the polyphonic.

Basso Continuo. "Continuous bass." A seventeenth- and eighteenth-century style of writing for keyboard instruments in which the music showed only a melody line and a bass line. Under the bass line were numbers and symbols that guided the performer in creating harmonies built on those notes, giving the player great latitude in "realizing" the *basso continuo.* In performance, the bass line was played by the keyboard player's left hand and a bass instrument, such as the cello. Also called figured bass or thoroughbass.

Canon. A composition, or section of a composition, in which all the parts have the same melody, but start it at different times. It is the strictest form of polyphony.

Cantabile. In a smooth, singing style.

Cembalo. Italian for "dulcimer." The Italian word for harpsichord, however, is *clavicembalo* ("keyed dulcimer"), which is usually shortened to *cembalo.* In common usage, therefore, *cembalo* means harpsichord.

Classicism. The period in music that followed the Baroque in the mid-eighteenth century and continued until the early nineteenth century and the emergence of the Romantic style. Classical music is, in general, characterized by restraint, objectivity, balanced proportions, nonprogrammatic music, and close adherence to the standard musical forms.

Clavicembalo. "Keyed dulcimer." Italian name for the harpsichord. The word is often shortened to *cembalo.*

Clavier. A general term for a keyboard instrument.

Counterpoint. A musical texture that is built up of two or more relatively independent melodic lines. The adjective form is *contrapuntal.*

Development. See *Sonata Form.*

Exposition. See *Sonata Form.*

Figured Bass. See *Basso Continuo.*

Fugue. A form of imitative counterpoint in which a short melody, the subject, is stated and then taken up in succession by other instruments or other parts on a keyboard instrument.

Hammerklavier. Literally "hammer keyboard." The old German term for the piano as distinct from the harpsichord.

Harpsichord. A very popular keyboard instrument of the sixteenth through the eighteenth century in which the sounding strings are plucked rather than struck, as in the more modern piano.

Neoclassicism. A contemporary musical style that embraces the Classical ideals of Haydn and Mozart, but presents them in twentieth-century terms.

Neoromanticism. A contemporary musical style that embraces the ideals of nineteenth-century Romanticism, but presents them in twentieth-century terms.

Polyphony. A word meaning "many sounds." A musical texture made up of apparently independent melodic lines that fit together harmonically. Essentially synonymous with counterpoint.

Program Music. Music with extramusical connections or associations that uses sound to describe scenes, people, events, moods, and so on.

Recapitulation. See *Sonata Form.*

Romanticism. A style of music predominant during the nineteenth century that stressed freedom, expressivity, imagination, individuality, and subjective emotionalism.

Rondo. A musical form with one principal theme that is usually repeated three times, with the repetitions separated by contrasting interludes.

Rubato. A performance style characterized by flexibility of tempo and rhythm; musical give-and-take.

Sonata. From the Italian verb *sonare,* "to sound." The term arose at the end of the sixteenth century to describe music written in a specifically instrumental style, in contrast with the primarily vocal cantata.

A sonata is generally an instrumental composition for one or two instruments in three or four separate, though related, movements (one- and two-movement sonatas, however, are not that rare), which differ in speed, rhythm, and key.

The early sonatas were for string instruments with a *basso continuo* part for harpsichord. One popular form was the trio sonata, which required four performers—two violinists playing the melody part, a cellist playing the bass line, and a harpsichordist also playing the bass line and filling in the harmonies. By the late eighteenth century, though, the term was usually restricted to music for one or two instruments; larger works were called trios or quartets.

A three-movement sonata usually follows this sequence:
1. Extended, weighty, fast, in sonata form
2. Slow, expressive, songlike
3. Fast and lively

Four-movement sonatas usually have an additional movement just before the last; most often it is quite brief—either a stately minuet or a gay scherzo.

Sonata or Sonata-Allegro Form. The most ubiquitous of all formal organizations in the sonata repertoire; used for practically every first movement, as well as a good percentage of subsequent ones.

The form has three major parts:

Exposition. Introduction of the themes: the first, or principal, theme, which often tends to be strong and forceful; the second, or subsidiary, theme, which is usually contrasting in character and key; the third, or closing theme, which is sometimes called the codetta. The music frequently directs the players to repeat the exposition, but this is not always observed in performance.

Development. A working out of the thematic material from the exposition. There is no limit on what the composer can do in this section, including fragmenting the melodies, combining them in different ways, expanding the melodies, casting them in new rhythms or harmonies, and almost invariably, building to the climax of the entire movement.

Recapitulation. The return of the themes from the exposition, usually somewhat shortened and with other modifications, and almost always with the second theme now in the same key as the first.

The three basic parts of sonata form are sometimes preceded by an introduction, separated by transitions, and followed by a concluding coda.

Sonata da Camera. "Chamber sonata." Music suitable to be played in a salon, consisting of a series of separate movements, each in a traditional dance rhythm. Most works of the sonata da camera type are called *suites* or *partitas,* rather than sonatas.

Sonata da Chiesa. "Church sonata." Music suitable to be played in church, consisting of a series of separate movements in a serious, abstract style. Typically there are four movements: A slow, introductory movement; a fast, fugal movement; a slow, expressive, and often melancholy movement; and a lively concluding movement. Most sonatas in the modern repertoire are closer to the sonata da chiesa than to the sonata da camera.

Sonatina. A composition similar to a sonata, but usually shorter and simpler in construction.

Theme and Variations. A musical form in which a simple theme is stated and then repeated a number of times with changes that add variety, but do not fully conceal the original melody, its rhythms, or its harmonies.

Thoroughbass. See *Basso Continuo.*

Twelve-Tone Method. An approach to musical composition devised in the 1920s by Arnold Schoenberg that eliminates any feeling of key or tonality by treating all twelve tones of the octave as equals. The twelve tones are first arranged in a tone row with no repetition of any of the notes. The tone row is then used both horizontally as melody, and vertically as harmony. In addition, the tone row may be reversed, inverted, or inverted *and* reversed.

Discography

Note: All of the recordings listed on this discography are of compact discs (CDs), a number of which are still available on long-playing records (LPs). In the few cases where a CD is not available, an LP is listed; the LP is indicated by the symbol #.

BACH, JOHANN SEBASTIAN
Flute Sonatas. Rampal, Pinnock. 2-CBS M2K-39746
Viola da Gamba Sonatas. Harnoncourt, Tachezi. 2-Teldec 48241 AG
Violin Solo Sonatas. Milstein. 2-Deutsche Grammophon 423294-2 GCM2
Violin Sonatas. Huggett, Koopman. 2-Philips 410401-2 PH2

BARBER, SAMUEL
Sonata for Cello and Piano, Op. 6. King, Jensen. Music & Arts CD-603
Piano Sonata, Op. 26. Browning. Desto 7120 #

BARTÓK, BÉLA
Sonata for Piano. Evans. Gasparo 211 (CX) #
Sonata for Solo Violin. Menuhin. Angel CDH-69804
Sonatas for Violin and Piano. Kremer, Smirnov. Hungaroton HCD-11655

BEETHOVEN, LUDWIG VAN
Cello Sonatas. Ma, Ax. 2-CBS M2K-42446
Piano Sonatas. Brendel. 11-Philips 412575-2 PH11
Violin Sonatas. Oistrakh, Oborin. 4-Philips 412570-2 PH4

BERG, ALBAN
Piano Sonata, Op. 1.   Cherkassky.   Nimbus NI-5021

BLOCH, ERNEST
Piano Sonata.   Shaulis.   CRI S-295 #
Sonata No. 1 for Violin and Piano.   Weilerstein Duo.   Arabesque Z-6605
Sonata No. 2 for Violin and Piano, "Poème mystique."   Weilerstein Duo.   Arabesque Z-6606

BRAHMS, JOHANNES
Cello Sonatas.   Harrell, Ashkenazy.   London 414558-2 LH
Clarinet Sonatas.   Stoltzman, Goode.   RCA 60036-2-RG
Piano Sonatas.   Zimerman.   2-Deutsche Grammophon 423401-2 GH2
Violin Sonatas.   Perlman, Ashkenazy.   Angel CDC-47403

CHOPIN, FRÉDÉRIC
Sonata for Cello and Piano, Op. 65.   Starker, Neriki.   Denon C37-7812
Piano Sonata No. 1, Op. 4.   Ashkenazy.   2-London 421035-2 LH2
Piano Sonata No. 2, Op. 35. "Funeral March."   Horowitz.   CBS MK-44797
Piano Sonata No. 3, Op. 58.   Perahia.   CBS MK-37280

CLEMENTI, MUZIO
Piano Sonata, Op. 40, No. 2.   Faini.   Spectrum 176 #
Piano Sonata, Op. 50, No. 3.   Newmark.   Folkways 3342 #

COPLAND, AARON
Sonata for Violin and Piano.   Laredo, Schein.   Desto 6439 #

CORELLI, ARCANGELO
Sonatas for Violin and Bass or Harpsichord, Op. 5, Nos. 1–6.   Kovacs, Banda, Sebestyen.   Fidelio 3318 #
Violin and Harpsichord Sonata, Op. 5, No. 12, "La Folia."   Purcell Quartet members.   Hyperion CDA-66226

DEBUSSY, CLAUDE
Sonata for Cello and Piano. Rostropovich, Britten.— London 417833-2 LH
Sonata for Violin and Piano.   Heifetz, Bay.   RCA AGM1-4952 #

FAURÉ, GABRIEL
Cello Sonatas.   Igloi, Benson.   CRD-3316
Violin Sonatas.—   Mintz,   Bronfman.—   Deutsche   Grammophon   423065-2 GH

FRANCK, CÉSAR
Violin Sonata.   Perlman, Ashkenazy.   London 414128-2 LH

GRIEG, EDVARD
Sonata for Cello and Piano, Op. 36.   Rostropovich, Richter.   Music & Arts CD-283
Piano Sonata, Op. 7.   Cherkassky.   Nimbus NI-5090
Violin Sonatas.   Sitkovetsky, Davidovich.   Orfeo C-047831A

HANDEL, GEORGE FRIDERIC
Sonatas for Flute, Op. 1.   Rampal, Veyron-Lacroix.   2-Odyssey YT-32371,2 (Cassette tape)
Sonatas for Oboe, Op. 1.   Roseman, Brewer.   Elektra/Nonesuch H-71339 #
Sonatas for Violin, Op. 1.   Suk, Ruzickova.   Denon CO-7053

HAYDN, FRANZ JOSEPH
Piano Sonata, WUA 33.   Ax.   CBS MK-44918
Piano Sonatas, WUA 58–62.   Gould.   2-CBS M2K-36947

HINDEMITH, PAUL
Sonata for Alto Horn and Piano, 1943.   J. & T. S. Barrows. Golden Crest S-7043
Sonata for Bassoon and Piano, 1938.   Grossman, Hokanson.   Coronet 2741
Sonata for Solo Cello, Op. 25. No. 3.   Sylvester.   Desto 7169
Sonatas for Cello and Piano.   Steiner, Berfield.   Orion 647 #

Sonata for Clarinet and Piano, 1939.— Forest, Tupas.— *Lyrichord 715* #

Sonata for Flute and Piano, 1936. Di Tullio, Mayorga. *GSC 3*

Sonata for Harp, 1939. Laughton. *GSC 5*

Sonata for 'Horn and Piano, 1939. Neal, Carno. *Desto 7206* #

Sonata for Oboe and Piano, 1938.— Lucarelli, Hrynkiv.— *Lyrichord 7320* #

Sonatas for Organ. Pecsi. *Hungaroton SLPX-12137* #

Sonata for Piano, 1936 (No. 3). Tupas. *Lyrichord 715* #

Sonata for Piano, 4 Hands, 1942. T. & R. Grunschlag. *CRI SD-472*

Sonata for Trombone and Piano, 1941. Shuman, Hambro. *Golden Crest 7011* #

Sonata for Trumpet and Piano, 1939. Tarr, Westenholz. *Bis 152* #

Sonata for Tuba and Piano, 1955. Bobo, Grierson. *Crystal S-125* #

Sonatas for Viola Solo. Kashkashian. *3-ECM 833309-1*

Sonatas for Viola and Piano. Kashkashian, Levin. *3-ECM 833309-2*

Sonata for Viola d'Amore and Piano, Op. 25, No. 2. Martin, Erhard. *Thorofon MTH-238*

Sonata for Violin and Piano, Op. 11, No. 1. Oistrakh, Yampolsky. *Monitor MCS-2009E* #

Sonata for Violin and Piano, 1935. Veselka, Dratvova. *Simax PS-1026* #

IVES, CHARLES
Piano Sonata No. 1. Henck. *Wergo 60-10150*

Piano Sonata No. 2, "Concord, Mass." Kalisch. *Elektra/Nonesuch H-71169* #

Violin Sonatas. Zukofsky, Kalisch. *2-Elektra/Nonesuch HB-73025* #

KODÁLY, ZOLTÁN
Sonata for Cello Solo, Op. 8. Starker. *Delos DCD-1015*

Sonata for Cello and Piano. Perenyi, Jando. *Hungaroton HCD-31046*

LISZT, FRANZ
"Dante" Sonata. Browning. Delos DCD-3022
Sonata in B minor. Watts. Angel CDC-47381

MENDELSSOHN, FELIX
Cello Sonatas. King, Moeling. Music & Arts CD-228
Organ Sonatas. Fagius. 2-Bis 156/7 #
Piano Sonata, Op. 6. Artymiw. Chandos CD-8326
Piano Sonata, Op. 105. Leconte. Ophelia OP-67104
Violin Sonata, Op. 4. Mintz, Ostrovsky. Deutsche Grammophon 419244-2 GH

MOZART, WOLFGANG AMADEUS
Piano Sonatas. Barenboim. 6-Angel CDCF-47335
Violin Sonatas, K. 296, 305 (293d), 306 (300e). Perlman, Barenboim. Deutsche Grammophon 415102-2 GH
Violin Sonatas, K. 301 (293a), 302 (293b), 303 (293c), 304 (300c). Perlman, Barenboim. Deutsche Grammophon 410896-2 GH
Violin Sonatas, K. 376 (374d), 377 (374e). Perlman, Barenboim. Deutsche Grammophon 419215-2 GH
Violin Sonatas, K. 378 (317d), 379 (373a), 380 (374f). Luca, Bilson. 2-Elektra/Nonesuch 79070-1 (D) #
Violin Sonatas, K. 454, 481, 526. Luca, Bilson. 2-Elektra/Nonesuch 79112-2

POULENC, FRANCIS
Sonata for Cello and Piano. Dobrinsky, Rabinovich. Calliope 1852 #
Sonata for Clarinet and Bassoon. Gigliotti, Garfield. Golden Crest 4115 #
Sonata for Clarinet and Piano. De Peyer, Pryor. Chandos CHAN-8526
Sonata for Two Clarinets. De Peyer, Simenauer. Musicmasters 60040W/41M #
Sonata for Flute and Piano. Wincenc, Schiff. Musicmasters 20004H #
Sonata for Oboe and Piano. Lucarelli, Hrynkiv. Lyrichord 7320 #

Sonata for Piano Four Hands. Tanyel, Brown. *Chandos CHAN-8519*

Sonata for Two Pianos. Tanyel, Brown. *Chandos CHAN-8519*

Sonata for Violin and Piano. Tarack, Hancock. *CCC 70 (Cassette Tape)*

PROKOFIEV, SERGEI

Sonata for Cello and Piano, Op. 119. Rostropovich, Richter. *Monitor MCS-2021E #*

Sonata for Flute and Piano, Op. 94. Galway, Argerich. *RCA LRK1-5095 (Cassette Tape)*

Piano Sonatas, Nos. 1–5. Nissman. *Newport Classic NCD-60092*

Piano Sonata No. 6, Op. 82. Cliburn. *RCA 7941-2-RG*

Piano Sonata No. 7, Op. 83. Bronfman. *CBS MK-44680*

Piano Sonata No. 8, Op. 84. Bronfman. *CBS MK-44680*

Piano Sonata No. 9, Op. 103. Richter. *Monitor MC-2034 #*

Sonata for Solo Violin, Op. 115. Lefkowitz. *Laurel 134 #*

Sonatas for Violin and Piano. Mintz, Bronfman. *Deutsche Grammophon 423575-2 GH*

Sonata for Two Violins, Op. 56. D. & I. Oistrakh. *Monitor MCS-2058 #*

RACHMANINOFF, SERGEI

Sonata for Cello and Piano, Op. 19. Harrell, Ashkenazy. *London 414340-2 LH*

Piano Sonatas. Eresco. *Chant du Monde LDC 278734*

RAVEL, MAURICE

Sonata for Violin and Cello. Laredo, Robinson. *Second Hearing GS-9009*

Sonata for Violin and Piano. Oistrakh, Bauer. *Philips 420777-2 PM*

Sonatine for Piano. Argerich. *Deutsche Grammophon 419062-2 GGA*

SCARLATTI, DOMENICO

Sonatas for Harpsichord (Various). Kipnis. *Angel CDM-69118*

Sonatas for Harpsichord (Various). Pinnock. *CRD CD-3368*

SCHUBERT, FRANZ
Sonata for Arpeggione and Piano, D. 821. Rostropovich (cello), Britten. London 417833-2 LH
Piano Sonata, D. 784. Watts. Angel CDC-49094
Piano Sonatas. Kempff. 7-Deutsche Grammophon 423496-2 GX7
Violin Sonata, D. 574. Tarack, Hancock. Monitor MCS-2146 #
Violin Sonatas (Sonatinas), D. 384, 385, 408. Kwalwasser, Wingreen. CCC 59 (Cassette Tape)

SCHUMANN, ROBERT
Piano Sonata No. 1, Op. 11. Ashkenazy. London 421290-2 LH
Piano Sonata No. 2, Op. 22. Perahia. CBS MK-44569
Piano Sonata No. 3, Op. 14. Horowitz. RCA ARK1-1766 (Cassette Tape)
Violin Sonatas.— Kremer, Argerich.— Deutsche Grammophon. 419235-2 GH

SCRIABIN, ALEXANDER
Piano Sonatas. Laredo. 3-Elektra/Nonesuch 73035-1 #

SHOSTAKOVICH, DMITRI
Sonata for Cello and Piano, Op. 40. Rostropovich, Shostakovich. Monitor MCS-2021E #
Piano Sonata No. 2, Op. 61. Plagge. Simax PSC-1036
Sonata for Viola and Piano, Op. 147. Uscher, Sternfield. Musicmasters 20055W #
Sonata for Violin and Piano, Op. 134. Oistrakh, Richter. Melodiya MFCD-909

STRAUSS, RICHARD
Sonata for Cello and Piano, Op. 6. Guye, Lively. Gallo CD-468
Sonata for Piano, Op. 5. Gould. CBS MK-38659
Sonata for Violin and Piano, Op. 18. Zukerman, Neikrug. Philips 420944-2 PH

STRAVINSKY, IGOR
Piano Sonata (1924). P. Serkin. New World NW-344-2

Sonata for Two Pianos. Jacobs, Oppens. Elektra/Nonesuch H-71347 #

VIVALDI, ANTONIO

Sonatas for Cello and Harpsichord. Hanani, Party, Gummere. Orion 618 (Cassette Tape)

Sonatas for Musette, Vielle, Flute, Oboe, or Violin, Op. 13, RV. 54–59, "Il pastor fido." Rampal, Veyron-Lacroix. RCA AGK1-4366 (Cassette Tape)

Sonata for Oboe and Harpsichord, RV. 53. Goritzki, Dahler, Sax. Claves D-901 (Cassette Tape)

Sonata for Recorder and Harpsichord, RV. 52. Harsanyi, Sarkozy. White Label HRC-045

Sonatas for Violin and Harpsichord, Op. 2. Ricci, Nesbitt, Bassett. 2-Etcetera ETC-2007 #

Sonatas for Violin and Harpsichord, RV. 2, 6, 25, 29. Boston Museum Trio. Harmonia Mundi HMA-190-1088

MELVIN BERGER is the author of a number of books on musical subjects, and is program annotator for several symphonic and chamber organizations. He has a B.M. from the Eastman School of Music, an M.A. from Teacher's College, Columbia University, and is an Associate of London University. He has written liner notes for RCA Records, contributed articles to *World Book,* directed chamber music programs at Ball State University and Silvermine Guild, and taught at the City University of New York. At present, he is writing, performing as a chamber music violist, and lecturing in the New York City area.